Microelectronics

Technology and
the Working Class

# Microelectronics

# Capitalist Technology and the Working Class

## CSE Microelectronics Group

CSE Books
55 Mount Pleasant
London WC1X 0AE

Microelectronics
was first published by CSE Books,
55 Mount Pleasant, London WC1X 0AE
in July 1980.

*British Library Cataloguing in Publication Data*
Conference of Socialist Economists
*Microelectronics Group*
Microelectronics
1. Labour supply
2. Microelectronics — Economic aspects
I. Title
331.1   HD5706

ISBN 0 906336  16 3
ISBN 0  906336 17 1 Pbk

Typeset and designed by
Calvert's North Star Press (TU) Ltd.
55 Mount Pleasant, London WC1X 0AE

Printed by Blackrose Press, London EC1R 0AT.

# Preface

This book was written collectively by the CSE Microelectronics Group between the late summer of 1979 and May 1980. We have tried to produce a concrete analysis of the impact of microelectronics on certain sectors of the British economy during the present period of restructuring. In doing so we have looked at the role technology plays within the social and economic relations of capitalism in Britain today.

In the opening chapter we outline the current period as one of capitalist restructuring following the end of the post-war boom in 1974. Capital needs to regain command over the labour process and to increase productivity in order to raise profits; technology plays a key role in this process.

We then look at the main characteristics of the production of microprocessors and micromemories themselves, highlighting the sexual and international divisions of labour imposed and orchestrated by capital. In chapter 3 we try to outline how microprocessors work and in chapter 4 we examine the conditions under which the programs which run the microprocessors are produced.

The necessity for managements to control and co-ordinate an increasingly detailed division of labour, and the growth of public and private sector industries, have led to the establishment of larger and larger offices. The office has become a major source of employment, especially for women. It has also become a major cost for capital, and in chapter 5 we examine the attempt to increase productivity by replacing the patriarchal relations of control in the office with those more familiar on the shop floor.

Next we look at five aspects of production and the ways in which workers in these sectors are reacting to the growing impact of microelectronics. In chapter 11 we concentrate on the banking system and outline the increasing problems facing bank workers with the introduction of automated money-handling devices.

The capitalist state attempts to regulate, incorporate and repress working-class struggles and we examine the role microelectronics plays in this process in chapter 12. The application of microelectronics in the economy requires particular aptitudes within the workforce, and in chapters 13 and 14 we examine related trends in education and training.

Finally, we take a look at some approaches to alternative design. If workers are to fight for the application of microelectronic-based technologies which serve their interests, it is essential that they become involved in the design stage, and not be forced to accept technologies as they come.

Drafts of these chapters were written within the Group, and developed through a number of versions in Group discussions. We are grateful to *Red Notes* for contributing chapter 9 on the motor industry, and to Ken Green for chapter 6 on small batch production. We are also grateful to the many other people who contributed to the book through discussions inside and outside the Group. The final version has been produced by Jane Barker, Iain Brodie, Ruth Carter, Hazel Downing, Mike Duncun, Trevor Evans, Dave Kraithman, John Newson, Dennis Sharp, Dave Wield and Graham Winch. Disagreements within the Group are reflected within the book—not all of us would agree with every view expressed.

We hope that this book is only the start of a continuing process. There are many ommissions; in particular, the book concentrates on waged labour and so ignores the effect of microelectronics on unwaged labour in the home. In addition, we do not look at the problem of those who are losing their jobs and the debates about the so-called leisure society. Finally, because we have only just begun discussing these issues, we have not drawn any overall conclusions from the arguments which are presented in the following chapters. These questions will be raised in future meetings of the group; we hope, however, that this book will help the current struggle around these issues and we welcome other people to join us. We can be contacted through the Conference of Socialist Economists, 55 Mount Pleasant, London WC1.

Thanks to the comrades at CSE Books for their advice and support; to Adrienne Lee and Mary Kuper at Calvert's North Star Press for their patience and care despite the poor quality of our copy and repeated delays; and to the comrades in Leeds, especially Ruth and Hugo, whose generous hospitality ensured that the work of the Group was so much more pleasurable than it might otherwise have been.

31 May 1980.

# Contents

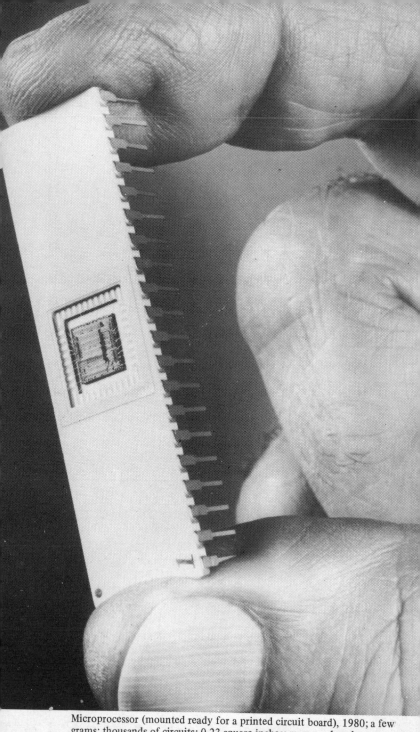

Microprocessor (mounted ready for a printed circuit board), 1980; a few grams; thousands of circuits; 0.23 square inches; mass produced.

# 1
# Capitalism
# & Technology

*Introduction*

The long economic boom that began after the second world war ended in 1974. This was partly overshadowed at the time in Britain by the dramatic events of that year. Conservative attempts to curb working-class power had culminated in an election based on the clear-cut class issue, 'Who Rules?'. The incoming Labour government only contained this level of militancy by conceding massive wage increases, several major new pieces of employment legislation, and the admission of a host of trade union officials onto existing and newly-created state institutions.

However, 1974 was a turning point for all the Western capitalist economies. Among the members of the Organisation of Economic Co-operation and Development (the organisation that represents all the main capitalist nations), industrial production grew continuously with only minor fluctuations throughout the post-war period, but between July 1974 and April 1975 it declined by 10% and unemployment leaped from a low of eight million during the boom to 15 million by the spring of 1975.

In Britain the value of shares on the London stock market slumped by 50% in 1974 — even more than during the celebrated crash of 1929. Industrial production declined for two successive years. All over the country workers were being laid off and made redundant, and unemployment reached its highest level since the 1930s. Although money wages did continue to rise, the real wage — what that money could actually buy — fell for the first time since the war. As the gap between the state's income and expenditure widened, it was faced with a fiscal crisis and for the first time since the welfare state was established after the war, plans were announced to cut its services.

This is the background against which microelectronic technology has been developed. This is a new technology that replaces transistor based electronics. Whereas in the past, complete electronic circuits were constructed from thousands of separate transistors, now they are etched onto tiny 'chips' of silicon. A complete central processor for a computer can be produced on a single chip. Equally important, memory chips can be used in place of the extremely bulky units that were used to store the instructions and data that are fed into the central processor. And because microelectronic circuits eliminate the need for wiring, they are far more reliable than transistor based circuits.

Microprocessors and micromemories can be mass produced at very low unit cost. This will have a major effect on future economic development. Computers will become smaller and cheaper and so are likely to be used far more widely than at present. Big computers will become more powerful, and so it will be possible to use them for much broader applications than at present. Microelectronic technology will also give rise to a whole range of new consumer products and provide the basis for redesigning many existing ones. But the main impact will be on the nature of work.

Microelectronics is being used to develop technology that will revolutionise factories, offices and many other working environments. Such technology could provide a powerful means of reducing the mind-numbing drudgery to which most workers are condemned for over half their waking lives. It could be used to end the appallingly dangerous and unhealthy conditions that so many workers are still forced to endure in the final quarter of the twentieth century. However, the studies in this book indicate that this is not why companies either produce or use microelectronic technology, whatever their public claims.

There are two broad approaches to explaining the development of new technology. One is basically technological, the other identifies the social forces that are involved. The first concentrates on simply describing the *technical* aspects of innovations. There certainly are scientific and technical limits to what can be developed at a particular time, but an explanation that confines itself to technical factors will fail to grasp the social framework within which the tasks of any technology are set. For example, any record of technological change that failed to document the impact of war on the timing and shaping of innovations would be very incomplete. In this chapter it will be suggested that there is an even more important influence on the development of new technology in a capitalist society.

Capitalism depends on the existence of a class of waged workers that produces a surplus over and beyond the goods that it receives for its own consumption. This surplus is the source of capitalists' profit. Part of the profit will be used by the capitalists to keep themselves in the style to which they are accustomed, part will be re-invested to expand production and produce even more profit. However periods of profitable growth become blocked as workers develop ways of resisting management discipline at work, and of building their strength in the related struggle over the size of their wage. It is this situation that provokes an urgent search by capitalists for new technologies that can be used to overcome such bottle-necks. The extent to which capitalists can impose this technology on the working class will be crucial in determining the basis for any subsequent period of profitable growth.

Eniac, 1946; 30 tons; 18,000 valves; hand built by scientists.

## The cycles of capitalist growth

Because our memories were dominated for many years by the experience of the post-war boom, there was a tendency for many people, including most economists, to take continual economic growth for granted. This has obviously been shaken by what has happened in the last few years, especially as the seriousness of the present situation is now being emphasised to justify large cuts in state services and the need for stringent wage restraint. Even so, the present recession is still usually presented as a deviation from a normal pattern of expansion.

In fact, all the Western capitalist economies have developed through the cycles that have lasted for about 50 years. Since the rise of industrial capitalism in Britain nearly 200 years ago, long booms that have lasted for about 25 years have been followed by long depressions of roughly the same duration. These cycles were documented in the 1920s by the Soviet economist, N. D. Kondratieff. He recorded the movement of wages, selected prices and the rate of interest, first for Britain and then for other countries as capitalist production developed in them. The existence of such long cycles has clearly been borne out since the 1920s by the way the inter-war depression was followed by the post-war boom that has now also come to an end.

Each long boom has been closely associated with the growth of one or more particular industries, as is illustrated for Britain in Figure 1.1. In the depressions that followed, it was these industries

*Figure 1.1*: Long Booms and Associated Industries

| Dates | Industry | |
|-------|----------|---|
| 1790-1815 | Cotton | Mechanisation of spinning |
| 1848-1873 | Textiles | Mechanisation of spinning and weaving |
| | Engineering | Production by machine of textile machinery, steam engines and locomotives |
| 1896-1921 | Engineering | Batch production semi-automatic machinery using of machines; marine engineering; motor car |
| | Electrical | |
| | Chemical | Rise of science based industries |
| | Steel | Bulk production |
| 1945-1974 | Motor Cars | |
| | Mechanical and Electrical Consumer durables | Assembly-line mass production |
| | Petro chemicals | Continuous-flow process production |

that generally suffered most markedly from decline and low profitability, whereas, at the same time, the industries that would play a leading role in the next boom were already developing. This was true in the 1930s of the motor and consumer durable industries: Coventry and the new industrial estates in West London were growing rapidly in contrast to the old centres of heavy engineering and shipbuilding in Scotland and the North East of England which bore the brunt of the depression. A similar situation exists at present, as sectors of the economy based on microelectronics are growing, while much of the motor industry is undergoing a protracted crisis.

## Production for profit

This cyclical pattern of development is undoubtedly the outcome of many factors. It is noticeable, for instance, how the cycles correspond broadly with major shifts in the structure of the world economy and the development of the state. More research is necessary to explain the duration of the cycles, but the key to their cause seems to lie in the class relations of a capitalist economy.

In a capitalist economy, the means of production – the factories, machinery and raw materials that provide the basis of material life – are nearly all owned by a small part of the population, the capitalist class. The existence of this capitalist class depends on the creation and maintenance of a class of workers who must sell their ability to work, their labour-power, for a wage.

Capitalists employ workers to transform raw materials into finished commodities that can then be sold at a profit. The value of the commodities is determined by the average labour-time that is necessary to produce them in a particular society. The value of the means of production that are used up in the production process is transferred to the commodity and new value is added by labour. Part of the new value will pay for the workers' wages, the other part is surplus value which is the source of the capitalists' profit. Effectively, workers just work part of the time (necessary labour-time) for themselves; during the rest of the time (surplus labour-time) they perform unpaid labour for the capitalist. However, because the wage appears to be paid for all the time spent at work, the source of profit is obscured.

The aim of capitalist production is to produce as much surplus value as possible, and until the second quarter of the nineteenth century the main way capitalists did this was by compelling their workers to work longer hours so as to prolong surplus labour-time.

But this had its limits. The day has only 24 hours and workers must spend at least some time eating and sleeping if they are to work the next day. More important, workers' opposition to this super-exploitation became so militant and widespread that legal limits had to be imposed on the length of the working day before the continued existence of the whole system was threatened.

Increasingly, those capitalists who could afford the necessary investment relied on transforming the labour process in which their workers were employed. By increasing workers' productivity, capitalists could reduce the quantity of labour needed to produce each commodity and so cut their costs. The real breakthrough was the introduction of machinery.

Machinery was first applied to cotton spinning at the end of the eighteenth century, and the extraordinary increase in productivity that resulted was the basis of the first long boom. The long booms that have occurred since then have each been based on the application of fundamentally new production techniques in other parts of the economy.

The capitalists who pioneer a new technique can initially achieve much higher profits, although such super-profits will become less marked as other capitalists are forced to adopt the new method too if they want to stay in business, and prices will fall to reflect the new, lower value. But there is also a further advantage which accrues to all capitalists as a result of a general increase in productivity. If wage goods can be produced more cheaply, then the same working-class standard of living will be associated with less necessary labour-time. Out of the same number of hours of work, more time will be spent on surplus labour. Even if workers succeed in winning a wage increase or shorter hours, it is still possible for the amount of surplus value that is produced to increase.

However, the success of this process tends to undermine itself. During a boom, profits will be re-invested to expand production. Additional machinery is generally similar to that already in use, rather than of a fundamentally new design. But the machinery is likely to incorporate a steady stream of improvements, and so less labour will be required to produce the same level of output. If production grows even more rapidly than productivity, then the total number of workers employed could still increase. However, capitalists will be investing a larger and larger proportion of their capital in machinery and raw materials and a smaller and smaller proportion in value-creating living labour. The outcome is that in the course of a long boom there is a tendency for the rate of profit (the amount of profit divided by the amount of capital invested) to fall.

## Workers' resistance

Capitalists experience the tendency of the rate of profit to fall as a need to rationalise and cut their costs. They therefore attempt to increase the intensity and productivity of the work of their employees. However, in attempting to do this capitalists are forced to confront the organised strength of the working class and in the course of a boom, conditions become more favourable for workers to resist capitalist demands.

Capitalists employ workers because they are necessary to produce a profit. As with any other commodity that they pay for, capitalists would like to be able to do as they choose with labour-power. What they want from workers is continuous work of the greatest possible intensity. But capitalist management has to find some way of enforcing this.

As far as workers are concerned, they go to work for a capitalist because it's the only way they can get the money that is necessary to live. There is therefore economic pressure on workers to conform to the demands of management, since insubordination might lead to the sack. This is particularly true when there is a large pool of unemployed. However, as capitalists employ a growing number of workers in a boom, the prospect of unemployment becomes less threatening.

In any job that depends on workers' skills, workers have to exercise some control over the labour process and this is a source of power that can be used against management. If only workers understand how a job is done, then management is not in a position to exercise detailed control over it.

The development of new technology has been one of the most important means that management has used to break workers' strength. When a machine incorporates the skills that were previously exercised by a worker, then the worker is deprived of this source of power, and management can use the machine to regulate the speed and intensity of its operators' work.

However, subordination is never established once and for all. Although management introduces technology to increase its control over the labour process, when workers find their feet in the new situation they set about rebuilding their strength. If workers are necessary for a capitalist labour process, they cannot be completely powerless. Since they observe the operation of any new technology at close quarters, day in and day out, they soon discover the weak points in a system. Any vulnerability is a source of strength that can be used to develop new forms of struggle.

The capitalist use of technology and workers' attempts to rebuild their strength are illustrated by the history of the metal-working industry. During each long boom, production has been based on techniques which were developed in the previous depression. In the first boom (1790-1815), the spinning machines and steam engines were built by artisans. In the next boom (1848-73), basic machines were used although they still required quite skilled labour. By the boom at the beginning of the twentieth century (1896-1921), semi-automatic machines that needed less-skilled labour had been introduced. And in the post-war boom (1945-74), assembly-line techniques using labour with hardly any training at all gave management an unprecedented degree of control over the organisation and intensity of work.

The artisans in the first boom had complete control over their work. In the next boom, engineering workers built up the Amalgamated Society of Engineers (founded 1851) to control the supply of skilled workers and boycott employers who refused their demands on working conditions and pay, and by 1871 they were strong enough to win the nine-hour day. In the years before the first world war, the exclusive organisation used to restrict the supply of skilled workers had to be broadened to include the less-skilled who would otherwise be used to break the union's strength, and from status-conscious conservatives engineering workers became some of the most active members of a very militant working-class movement. During the most recent boom, assembly-line workers developed forms of struggle that were often based on informal organisation in the plant rather than the official union, and by the late 1960s and early 1970s, car workers in particular had become strong enough to seriously limit management control. Management began searching for a technological solution, and cheap microelectronics are now providing the basis for automatic devices that can be used either instead of workers at key bottlenecks, or selectively, to try and isolate workers from each other and prevent successful organisation within a plant.

## Restructuring and the long depression

There is then on the one hand an underlying tendency for the rate of profit to fall in the course of a long boom. On the other hand, capitalist attempts to counter-act this through rationalisation are likely to be blocked by the working class. The outcome will depend on how successful workers are in developing forms of organisation and struggle that are appropriate to the particular period of capitalist development.

An actual fall in the rate of profit doesn't lead to a gradual decline in the economy because of the operation of the credit system. Companies raise capital through the stock market; they buy raw materials and sell finished products on credit; they depend on bank loans for shorter or longer periods. Consequently, future profits may well have been committed before they have been produced. When the rate of profit declines, capitalists are likely to try to meet their commitments by speculating in some commodity which is in limited supply. In 1974, the crisis was preceded by widespread speculation in property and raw materials. The result is that a stagnating growth of production is masked by an illusory growth of exchange based on over-extended credit.

When the crisis breaks, the weakest capitalists go bankrupt. As the economy contracts and commodities cannot be sold, other capitalists are forced to lay off workers. Unemployment increases and this makes it easier for capitalists to depress wages and for management to strengthen its authority over workers. The crisis is a disaster for individual capitalists since sometimes the existence of even the biggest companies is threatened. British Leyland only survived after 1974 because it was nationalised. However, crises have an important function in a capitalist economy. The least efficient enterprises are purged, and rationalisation is imposed as the price of survival.

In the long depressions that follow the crises, capitalists are forced to withdraw from the least profitable sectors of the economy and attempt to lay the foundations for a new period of profitable growth. This means ensuring that workers spend less time on necessary labour and more time producing surplus value. It means revolutionising productivity in those sectors of the economy that produce machinery and raw materials so that they become cheaper and capitalists will only need to invest a smaller proportion of their capital in means of production. It also means speeding up the time that it takes for capital to complete a circuit, from being advanced for means of production and labour power, through the production process to being sold so that the profit is realised and the capital reinvested to produce yet more profit. This will affect offices, the distribution system, transport and communications and many other sectors of the economy.

During depressions, therefore, capitalists are impelled to search for new forms of technology that can be used to restructure the economy. Above all, they have to be able to overcome their dependence on those sectors of the working class who have used their position in the economy to build sufficient strength to act as a

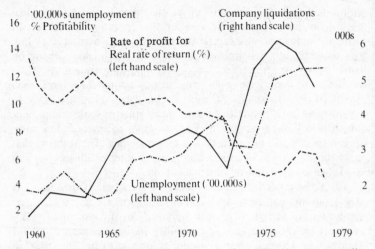

'00,000s unemployment
% Profitability

Company liquidations
(right hand scale)

Rate of profit for
Real rate of return (%)
(left hand scale)

Unemployment ('00,000s)
(left hand scale)

bottleneck. Since the introduction of new technology is usually resisted by workers, depressions tend to be periods of intense struggle in which capitalists are by no means assured of success in implementing the techology that has been developed.

During the third quarter of the nineteenth century, for example, the production of pig-iron became a major bottleneck in the long boom based on the production by machine of machines made of iron. The production of iron depended on highly skilled puddlers who formed balls of pasty, half-molten iron on top of a puddling furnace and then drew it off. They were well organised in skilled unions and repeated attempts to break their control by mechanising the process failed. The capitalist solution finally lay in bypassing the problem entirely and producing steel. Previously steel could only be produced in tiny quantities, but now, with the invention of several new production processes, it could be produced in bulk. The giant US steel industry grew on the basis of these new techniques, though their introduction was resisted by the skilled-workers' union which was finally broken after a long, and at times armed, struggle. In Britain, by contrast, workers' organisation not only survived the transition to steel production, but it broadened its base in the ensuing struggle to include less-skilled workers and workers succeeded in maintaining control over the labour process.

## Restructuring the working class

The composition of the working class that has been employed during each long boom has been different from that which was expelled during the previous depression. There have been two main elements in this process of recomposition.

Firstly, skilled workers who have been the most highly organised have been displaced by workers who have less training and who do not usually have the same organisational traditions. During the post-war boom there was a massive expansion in the employment of women workers. A substantial black working class was also created.

Secondly, there has been a shift in employment away from the direct process of production. This has involved an expansion of technical and office work, and the growth of the state as a major employer.

When technology is used to remove control of a labour process from the immediate workers, someone must be able to design and understand the new system. A few highly-skilled jobs are created, but once these tasks expand to employ more than just a tiny elite, the new jobs are themselves subjected to a division of labour and the more routinised parts of the work are separated out leaving those parts that continue to require much initiative concentrated in the hands of a few individuals. This separation of the process of conception from that of execution, even within the most technologically advanced sectors of the economy, has resulted in a polarisation between a few key personnel and a mass of routinised technicians.

Office work has expanded for several reasons. One is the need to look after the commercial and financial affairs of big companies. The size of companies has continually increased as profits have been reinvested to expand the scale of production and as a result of mergers and takeovers. A large number of office staff are needed to organise the transactions of a big company which may involve different plants, or even different countries.

Office work has also expanded as a result of attempts to shift knowledge and control away from the factory floor. In addition to using technology to accomplish this, capitalists have developed sophisticated techniques of work-study. These were first systematised at the turn of the twentieth century by F. W. Taylor, who called his new discipline scientific management. Taylorism, as it has become known, involves systematically studying a job, no matter how complex, in order to identify each type of task that must be performed. Once management has appropriated complete knowledge of a job, by documenting every possible variation that can occur, it is in a position to take command. Each worker can now be allocated just a detail to work on under strict management supervision. But once the immediate workers have been deprived of knowledge of the labour process, then every stage has to be monitored and recorded by management and this has meant duplicating the production process with a flow of paper in the office.

Office work has generally been organised on the basis of a division of labour in which managerial and executive work has been performed, predominantly by men, within a defined career structure, and the mass of routine clerical labour has been provided largely by women. Clerical work is labour intensive and much of the technology in use, like the typewriter, has remained basically unchanged for many years. This has caused a severe imbalance, because while office employment has grown and factory employment has declined, productivity has increased far more slowly in the office than in the factory. The office has become a bottleneck in the process of profitable growth and will therefore be a major target of restructuring in the current period of depression. Microelectronic technology is being developed that will make it possible to begin the process of automating the office.

The largest employer in Britain is now the state, and many of its workers are also involved in clerical work and other forms of labour intensive work in which productivity has been fairly stagnant. State workers were for many years very poorly paid, but by the late-1960s unionisation had begun to take place and in the course of a series of struggles these workers managed to win large wage increases. State workers now face cuts in the level of employment and attempts to increase their workload through rationalisation and increased management supervision. Arguments about the unproductive nature of state employment have been eagerly seized on to justify the cuts that are being made.

Such arguments illustrate how, in a period of restructuring like the present, there are not only attacks on the strength of the most well-organised sections of the working class, but also continued attempts to strengthen the divisions between different sections of the working class so as to undermine any possibility of collective struggle. The ideology of the male bread-winner is being revived to explain why women should bear the brunt of unemployment and there has been a growth of racist immigration legislation. Government economic policy is being used to divide employed from unemployed workers and to isolate those workers who do fight back by going on strike. It is in this atmosphere that anyone who does so much as pause to consider whether or not the introduction of new technology is in their best interest is immediately denounced as a Luddite.

# 2
# Hardware

The microelectronic industry spends a lot of time and effort trying to get across the message that its high technology products demand a corresponding high level of skill in the work force. Intel, the fourth biggest microelectronics producer in the world, said in its 1978 *Annual Report*: 'Our guiding principle is that, if Intel is to grow, its people must grow with its capabilities. A growth company must be, among other things, an educational institution.' And Motorola, the third biggest manufacturer, said one reason for building a micro-electronic memory manufacturing plant in Scotland was the skills in the work force. This chapter looks at the conditions under which workers in the microelectronic industry labour day in and day out to make a profit for their employers by producing microprocessors and micromemories, hardware, in one of the fastest growing industries in the world.

Many of the major companies in the microelectronic industry were founded and now have their headquarters in a valley 60 kilometres long just south of San Francisco, California, which, until twenty years ago, was bean fields and olive groves. Silicon Valley, as it has been dubbed after the basic material from which microelec-tronic circuits are made, has over 120 large companies each with 250 or more workers and a host of smaller firms either starting up or supplying specialist services to the bigger ones. Between them these firms employ over 190,000 workers. It is here, in Silicon Valley, that the majority of silicon chips made in the United States are manu-factured and where many of the most important breakthroughs in production technique and design have been made. Just over half the workers in the Valley have jobs maintaining the production equipment or within production itself.

A majority of these workers are women. Recent investigations into this almost totally non-unionised labour force by an American trade union have painted a telling picture of the average production worker. She is most probably Chinese, Mexican or Puerto Rican and English is her second language. She is somewhere between 18 and 30

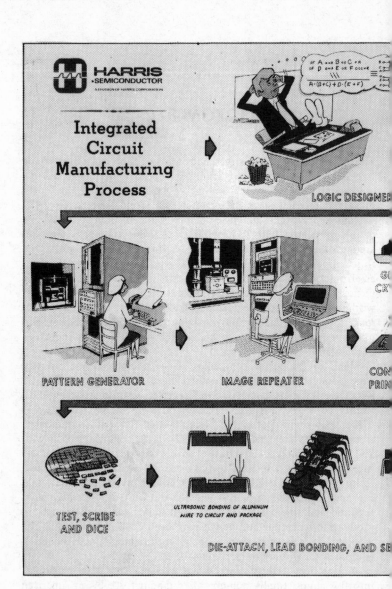

HARRIS
SEMICONDUCTOR
A DIVISION OF HARRIS CORPORATION

Integrated
Circuit
Manufacturing
Process

LOGIC DESIGNER

PATTERN GENERATOR

IMAGE REPEATER

CONTACT PRINT

TEST, SCRIBE AND DICE

ULTRASONIC BONDING OF ALUMINUM WIRE TO CIRCUIT AND PACKAGE

DIE-ATTACH, LEAD BONDING, AND SEAL

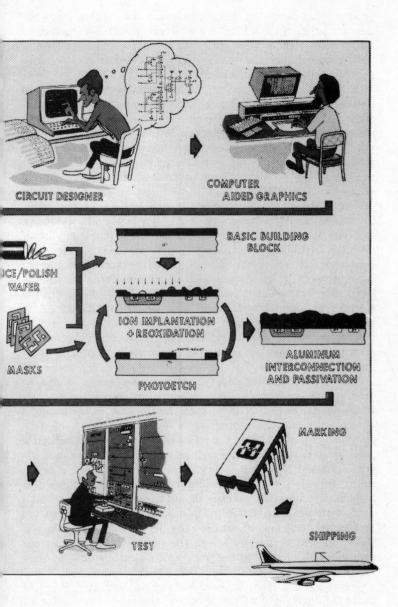

years old, has dependent children and has to pay for their care when they are either not at school or are too young for schooling because she works a 40-hour week. She is most probably on some form of welfare because her pay, at just over $5,000 a year, is either at or only just above the legal minimum.

She has no power to control the production process – all she can do is work at the speed dictated by the computer systems which control the very expensive capital equipment used in the various stages of microelectronic production. Without power her skills will not be recognised in money or status; the only recognition she will get is some job title on an embossed plastic card attached to her white coat. For the supervision of other workers, however, she will get a salary increase.

The production lines are housed in air-conditioned cabins where she will be exposed to chemicals of all types in the different manufacturing stages as the wafer of silicon, like a four-inch slice of salami, has hundreds of microscopic electronic circuits etched onto it. Side by side with organic solvents, she will be working with highly corrosive acids used to etch away unwanted deposits on the wafer as layer after layer of circuits are formed on it. In all, the production worker is surrounded by materials which will irritate the skin, cause rashes, dizziness, nausea and, when inspecting the wafers under a microscope, severe eye strain. The main production processes are monitored by computer systems which set the basic pace at which she will have to work.

She will be labouring under the direct management of men, to produce a microelectronic circuit designed by men for a company which will be owned by men. These men operate in the limelight of intense media fascination, where their ability to build fast-growing companies or design a denser and faster electronic circuit is given great prominence. One such man is Ted Hoff, who, as a 32-year-old research worker at Intel in 1969, worked out a design which, for the first time, would put the complete workings of a rudimentary computer processor on just one chip slightly less than a sixth of an inch long and an eighth of an inch wide. His design was adopted by the heads of the company, Robert Noyce and Gordon Moore, themselves industry heroes who had taken the now familiar path of breaking away at the height of their careers from an older company to form their own firm in the late 1960s.

Before forming Intel, Noyce and Moore had worked at Fairchild under the direction of William Shockley, winner of a Nobel prize for his work in the laboratory of the Bell Telephone Company which resulted in the first transistor in 1948. Before transistors, valves were the major electronic component – they were costly to make and un-reliable as well as consuming a lot of electrical energy and so getting very hot. Shockley and his colleagues stuck layers of electronic conducting material one on top of the other and, by passing a current through the device in certain ways, were able to control it like a switch. One transistor could substitute for a glass valve, was up to ten times smaller, took less power and was more reliable. The US Government poured millions of dollars into the development of transistors and in the first two years took the total world production of the new device for its military and space projects. Shockley moved to the West coast of the US and, with new capital from the Fairchild Camera and Instrument company, established a laboratory near Stanford University just south of San Francisco.

One of the most brilliant designers he recruited in the 1950s from Stanford was Robert Noyce. Noyce became part of a design team which, in the early 1960s, managed to put more than one transistor on the same small piece of silicon – integrating first two, then tens of transistors into complex circuit patterns and forming the technical basis of the integrated-circuit industry. In the early 1960s production methods were developed at Fairchild and the other blossoming microelectronic companies which put hundreds of transistors on a chip – what is now called small scale integration (ssi). Hoff's breakthrough in the late 1960s was implemented with pro-duction techniques which could etch 2,250 transistors on a chip – medium scale integration (msi). The standard memory chip in 1980 used over 100,000 transistors in the same area as the original single device – very large scale integration (vlsi).

A sexual division of labour, with women doing the production jobs and men the design and management, is one of the foundations of this industry. Another is an international division of labour.

## In search of cheap labour

The production capacity to build microelectronic devices for the general electronics market as well as the US Government has been kept inside the United States. But once the complete wafer, on which up to 600 individual chips will be made simultaneously, has been produced the wafer is cut up and each chip is mounted on its own base. Connections from the edge of the chip to pins have to be made so that the current to drive the chip and the signals to control it can flow from a board on which the chips will be mounted. Unlike the production of the completed wafer, this assembly job is labour-intensive. In 1963 the major microelectronics companies, led by

*Figure 2.1*: Mostek's years of superprofit – 1972-1974.

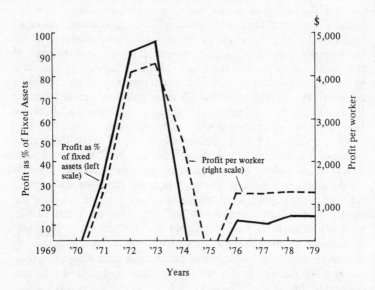

Fairchild, set out in search of the cheapest labour power they could find to perform these assembly and test functions. They found the labour power they were looking for in South East Asia and Fairchild broke the ground by establishing an assembly factory in the British colony of Hong Kong. The other major companies followed suit and, throughout the 1960s, Taiwan, South Korea and Singapore were firm favourites.

By the early 1970s Intel was building a thriving market in the US for its microprocessor and other companies were beginning to build computer memories from microelectronic devices instead of the older hand-threaded core memories. This new level of integration led to a new wave of expansion between 1972 and 1974, this time into Malaysia, Thailand, the Philippines and Indonesia. The workers used in these new plants, again mostly women, came from rural backgrounds and many of them had, before their employment in the US-owned plants, no experience of wage labour. By 1978, Malaysia, to take one example, had 69 microelectronic assembly plants, 20 of them owned by the biggest US companies. The country had become, a contemporary US Government report said, 'one of the major manufacturers of semiconductors in the world'. The value of the microelectronic components produced there grew from $382.9 million in 1976 to $500 million in 1977, an increase of 37%. And the big employers, like Motorola, Texas Instruments and RCA, had already gone onto three shift a day working.

The 300,000 women workers in these South East Asian plants, which are managed by American men sent out by the parent corporation, are non-unionised. They are the target for a constant barrage of sexist propaganda aimed at reinforcing an image of subservience and loyalty to the company. This propaganda exploits the traditionally defined attributes of femininity—passivity, submissiveness, sentimentality and sexual desirability—while creating a factory life-style separate from the society surrounding it. Discipline in the plants is strict, with workers assigned daily and monthly quotas which they labour to achieve during the eight-hour shifts from which they are allowed only 45 minutes rest in a working day.

Wages are highest in Hong Kong, about $5 a day, and lowest in the newer plants, such as those in Indonesia and the Philippines, where they are $0.80 and $0.86 a day respectively. A full working life for these women tends to be only about four years because over this time their eyesight will be ruined by looking through a microscope all day, wiring the edges of the chips to the pins. Once their eyesight deteriorates to the point where they fail one of the regular check-ups, these women who have been dragged out of their rural society to work for US bosses, serve them in another role by joining the growing population of prostitutes which is a constant feature of all South East Asian capitalist cities.

This labour force does not engage in the more traditional struggles of an organised working class for more pay, less work and better conditions. Their only permissible form of resistance is sporadic outbursts of hysteria, often given a religious expression, which can be used to halt production processes.

Apart from the internal factory discipline and the waves of new workers entering the city every day in search of work, the constant threat of unemployment keeps them working. When a recession hit the industry in 1974, 15,000 microelectronic workers in Singapore, a third of the microelectronic industry workforce on the island, was thrown out of work.

These workers are sexually, nationally and racially disadvantaged and from their powerless position unable to fight for better conditions, pay or status. Instead, since the late 1960s, capital has retained an initiative over them by constant and rapid change in the production process. The only skill they need have is manual dexterity, a skill which the US corporations say is the special gift of women. In this powerless position their role is to produce profit at an extraordinary rate compared with other industries.

## The superprofiteers

Every microelectronic company invests vast sums, between 5% and 9% of their turnover, in research and development looking for some technological breakthrough which will give it a unique product or a cheaper production process that will earn a massive profit before other producers can catch up. Mostek's return on assets and its profit earned from each worker through the 1970s are a clear example of this, as Table 2.1 shows. The years 1972 and 1973 are Mostek's period of superprofits—a short heyday when it extracted nearly $5,000 a year from each worker and made enough profit to completely replace its capital equipment as a result of its lead in micromemory products.

These are the levels of profit made from the labour of workers in the peripheral and metropolitan countries who are the workforce of the microelectronic industry. The sustained initiative that capital has successfully mounted in the industry has restructured the production processes to the point where such vast sums of money are needed to start up production that even large corporations cannot break into the market. These barriers against the entry of new capitals into the industry have been created both by the technical demands of production and also by capital's constant obsolescence of the production process. Technological advance is therefore aimed in two directions at once: to keep out new capitals and to keep the workforce unorganised and docile by constantly threatening labour's place in the production process in the next wave of technical advance.

Production is dominated by a handful of companies with plants in the United States, Western Europe, Japan and the capitalist enclaves remaining under imperialist control in South East Asia. These companies have a variety of backgrounds. Some of them, like the West German giant Siemens, have their roots in the older electrical industry formed in the late 19th century.

Another group of manufacturers was founded in the 1950s in the United States and Japan to take advantage of transistor technology, the biggest ones today being National Semiconductor and Texas Instruments. Computer, telecommunication and office product companies like IBM, Ferranti and the Dutch-based multinational Philips entered microelectronic production to secure a supply of devices for their own products. And, finally, there are the block of new-comers which, like Intel and then Mostek, were specially formed to exploit microelectronic technology in the mid- and late-1960s.

Between 1969 and 1972 Intel, which initially employed 200 workers, spent $3.85 million establishing its plant and equipment in Silicon Valley. Despite the need to do the design work before starting production, within months of its formation the majority of workers in Intel were women on the lower clerical and production grades. When this initial production capacity was being used to its full potential in 1972 just over $23 million worth of sales were generated from that $3.85 million capital investment and a profit of $3.1 million was made.

To establish a microelectronic production plant making chips to store 16,000 binary digits of data, in the early 1980s, cost an estimated investment of $8.5 million. About 2.5 million microelectronic devices could be produced a year from this equipment and each chip would sell on the market at about $8. Total annual sales from such a plant would be about $20 million.

By 1982 the capital needed to open a manufacturing line for 64,000-bit memory chips will have risen to $18 million and by 1985 it is estimated that this will have risen to $40 million for a plant producing microelectronic memories storing 256,000 binary digits. This, then, is the mounting barrier that companies have to surmount if they are to get into the industry.

The largest producer of microelectronics in the world is IBM. But, unlike almost every other manufacturer, IBM does not sell any of its chips to other companies—it uses them all in its own computer, telecommunications and office products.

The largest producer of chips which does sell them to other firms is Texas Instruments which sold $800 million worth of microelectronic devices in 1979. Motorola, whose sales grew at nearly 40% a year from 1976 to 1980, grossed around $450 million in the late 1970s.

Just as IBM believes it is essential to produce its own microelectronic components, so other large companies in industries which consume chips in their products have started to buy into the industry to secure their source. Mostek, the fastest growing chip manufacturer in the US during the 1970s, was taken over by the United Technologies multinational in 1979 and the French-based Schlumberger giant bought Fairchild for $397 million in the same year. In planning such takeovers, the multinational predators are always afraid that the key technologists—the designers of the circuits and the production methods—will leave before the multi-national has had time to exploit their skills. It is this group of key technologists, men like Hoff at Intel, which, by their power over the production processes, stand at the opposite end of the labour market from the South-East Asian assembly workers.

*Skilled workers*

The key technologists are highly paid and generally plough a lot of their salaries back into buying shares in the company at preferential rates. This is how they build the capital which they then use to form their own companies, as Noyce and others did with Intel. But as the barriers to entry mounts this path is being cut off and any new firms that do enter the industry are likely to be the subsidiaries of large multinationals in other industries which are buying their way into the market. The classic case in point is Exxon, the largest oil company in the world, which formed its own microelectronic production arm called Zilog in the mid-1970s.

All the companies in the industry spend something between 6% and 9% of their total sales revenue on research and development. In 1978, for instance, Intel spent $41 million. These resources are channelled into solving the problems faced in the design and manu-facture of future devices so that they consume less electrical power, give off less heat, store more data and process it faster—all at a lower cost. The key technologists believe themselves to be involved in purely technical work to which they relate with a spirit of pro-fessionalism and scientific adventure.

To them the technology is beneficial, they have no illusions about a neutral role for the technology benefits them, their children, their firm and the whole world all in one go. Even arguments about specific applications, such as weapons systems or enhanced sur-veillance, do not move them to examine their own practice and their relationship with capital. But where they have never been challenged is over the essential function that they perform for capital—a function which allows capital to obsolete the production process every four years and so retain an initiative over the labour force that has its production skills decomposed, its wages squeezed and its activities tightly disciplined.

As the barriers to entry mount, however, their own dream of becoming capitalists will fade and their own position as wage labourers will be reinforced. Indeed, during the 1970s, their own work was subject to speed-ups as any company that was left even slightly behind in the technology race could not reap the super-profits which were necessary to finance the next generation of plant.

# 3
# How it works

A computer is often thought of as a device with lots of flashing lights, switches and dials that can be controlled only by some super specialist. Explanations of how it works are often put in human terms: computers apparently 'go and check if something is ready', 'wait for an answer', 'decide whether something is right or wrong', or 'remember'. Using such terms to describe these machines only confuses our understanding of their place in society and mystifies the role of technology. By introducing some of the basic principles of computer technology we hope to contribute to a process of de-mystification. Microelectronic technology uses the same techniques and principles as the more general field of digital computing.

## The basic machinery

The actual task performed by a computer is the processing of data. Certain inputs are available: rates of pay, hours of work, a tempera-ture reading. The machine processes these items and gives an output like a pay slip or a signal to control a heater. This is done by following a precise, pre-planned program of instructions until all the required processing has been performed.

The program is produced by human effort, can be changed, and is an input into the computer (see section in this chapter on 'Instructing the Computer' and Chapter 4 on Software).

A computer consists basically of a central processor and a memory, as illustrated in figure 3.1. The memory stores the program and data while the central processor takes each instruction in turn and processes it. Input and output devices transfer data into and out of the computer. The most common device is the visual display unit (VDU) which looks like a TV screen with a typewriter keyboard. The keyboard is used to pass data into the machine while the screen displays the computer's output. Other devices allow the computer to take information from small cards or strips of paper tape. In both cases the information is coded by patterns of holes punched onto

*Figure 3.1*: The computer has four parts

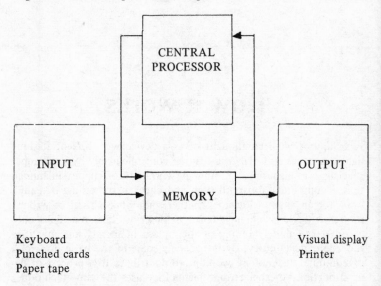

Keyboard
Punched cards
Paper tape

Visual display
Printer

the card or tape. Another common output device is the line printer which types output on to paper to give a permanent record. The central processor and memory, along with the various input and output devices are collectively known as hardware.

## The basic principles of hardware

For a computer to function a whole program has to be loaded into the machine. This coded program consists of various patterns of two digits, *0* and *1*, which is known as binary code. The numbers 0 to 9 are represented in binary as follows:

| | | | |
|---|---|---|---|
| 0 | *0000* | 5 | *0101* |
| 2 | *0001* | 6 | *0110* |
| 2 | *0010* | 7 | *0111* |
| 3 | *0011* | 8 | *1000* |
| 4 | *0100* | 9 | *1001* |

A two-digit system is used to represent numbers and letters in all digital computers. This is because the most elementary component of both the central processor and the memory is a tiny electronic switch that has two positions: ON and OFF. Each position is used to represent one of the two digits in the binary code.

The electronic switches within the central processor and memory units are connected to form two groups of components, *gates* and *flip-flops*. For this discussion we only need to consider the flip-flop, the basic element for representing data, and a special purpose switch, the tri-state switch, which is used to control the flow of data. The gates set up the various communication lines within the computer.

The flip-flop is the basic element of computer memory. It stores the value *0* or *1* by locking into the position ON or OFF. The best analogy to a flip-flop is a normal light switch that has to be physically pushed into one position or another and, once in that position, has to be physically pushed the other way in order to be changed. The flip-flop works similarly: a small electrical push (a pulse) will move the flip-flop to the position representing either *1* or *0*. The flip-flop stays in position even when the input ends so the last value input is stored. Only another electrical pulse will remove it.

The tri-state switch controls the flow of data by electronically connecting or disconnecting a line which is used to transfer the data. The switch connects the data line when a *1* is present on the control line, or disconnects it when a *0* is present, as shown in Figure 3.2. A bit of information, a single *1* or *0*, is therefore used in a computer both to represent a data value, as in a flip-flop, and to control the transfer of data, as on the control line of a tri-state switch.

*Figure 3.2*: The tri-state switch

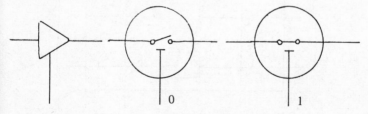

| The symbol to represent it | A *0* on the control line opens the switch while a *1* closes it allowing the data to transfer through. |

### Registers

Single flip-flops and tri-state switches are not very useful because instructions and data are represented by a row of *1*s and *0*s, while each flip-flop can store only one bit of information. Eight bits to-gether make one byte. To store one byte of information eight flip-flops have to be connected in a row. A byte of information can then be put on to the eight input lines so that one pulse to all the flip-flops will make them store the complete input pattern. Such a device is called a register. Its length depends on how many flip-flops are connected in a row.

The transfer of data into and out of the register can be controlled by using a tri-state switch in each input and output line as shown in Figure 3.3. If the control wires to each row of tri-state switches are connected together, a single *1* can control the whole row of input or output lines. The action of connecting the inputs or outputs is known as enabling and the enabling signals control the flow of data.

*Figure 3.3*: Controlling data into and out of a register

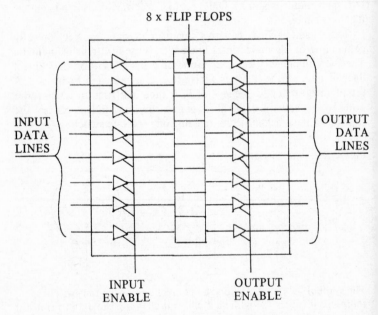

The central processor of a computer functions through trans-ferring complete bytes of information from one register to another and the enable lines make this possible. Data is transferred by connecting two registers together on a common set of lines, as illus-trated in Figure 3.4.

*Figure 3.4*: Two registers connected by common datalines

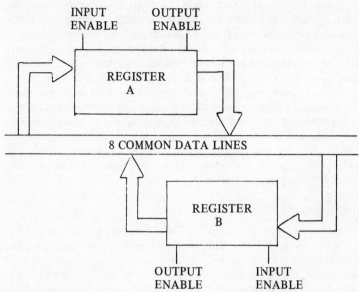

By enabling the output of register A and at the same time enabling the inputs to register B, a direct connection is made between them allowing the contents of register A to be transferred to register B.

A central processor will have up to 100 of these registers. There are also other special-purpose devices that can add together two coded numbers. As addition can provide the basis for all arithmetic operations, a single addition circuit can provide the basis of all the processing. All the units will be connected to the common lines, like the two registers above, and where necessary they will have enable lines. As the data lines are common, enabling any input will make a connection to any enabled output. It is this system that provides the control over data processing within the central processor.

A memory unit will consist of thousands of registers connected through common data lines to the central processor. The transfer of data, or an instruction, from the memory to the central processor is achieved by enabling the output of a memory register, and at the same time enabling the inputs to a central processor register.

*Microprocessors*

This limited discussion of hardware is intended to give an idea of how data is represented and controlled. While digital computers are very complex machines, it can be seen that they are made up of switches. With current techniques of etching tiny electronic switches on to silicon, it is possible to construct an entire central processor on one chip of silicon. This is a microprocessor.

But besides a central processor, a computer requires a memory unit as well as input and output devices. A microprocessor may cost less than £20, but a simple computer based on it will be more expensive as a result of the remaining hardware that is necessary. Computers of this sort are called microprocessor systems or microcomputers. As far as the users of computers are concerned, there is no difference between the working principles of a microprocessor-based computer and any other computer of equivalent power. The difference between microprocessor systems and other computers is their physical size and their price.

*Instructing the computer*

For the computer to follow or run a program, all the instructions have to be loaded into the computer memory through an input device. It is these programs, usually formed from thousands of instructions, that are collectively referred to as software. The instructins that form the program fall into two categories: those to directly manipulate and process data and those to control the sequence of processing. An example of a simple program using instructions that only manipulate data is:

1 LOAD 8        this moves data (the number 8) into the central processor.
2 SUBTRACT 3    this moves the number 3 into the central processor and subtracts it from 8.
3 OUTPUT        this feeds out the data from the central processor, the number 5 as 8 − 3 = 5.

Letters and symbols are easily handled by giving each one a numerical code; representing the alphabet in this way makes text handling a simple process. Such techniques provide the basis for word processors. In this way the LOAD and OUTPUT instructions can be used to transfer a letter from the memory into the central processor and then out via an output device. For example, to print out WORK HARDER on a screen, a set of instructions would have to load and then output each individual letter. The program would be something like:

1 LOAD W
2 OUTPUT
3 LOAD O

. .

. .

. .

18 LOAD E
19 OUTPUT
20 LOAD R
21 OUTPUT

The second group of instructions, those that control the sequence of processing data, give the computer its flexibility. The individual instructions do not directly operate on data. A typical example of this group of instructions is GO TO which is always followed by an instruction number, for example GO TO 2. Whenever the instruction is followed the computer always goes to instruction number 2 and carries on from there. Let us look at the usefulness of sequencing instructions by putting GO TO 2 as the fourth instruction on the subtraction program.

1 LOAD 8
2 SUBTRACT 3
3 OUTPUT
4 GO TO 2

On running the program, the processor will, as before, subtract 3 from 8 and then output the result 5, but when instruction 4 has been followed the computer will return to instruction 2. This will again subtract 3, giving −1, and so on to −4, −7, etc. This simple instruction shows how, by the addition of sequencing control, the program has completely changed. Without the instruction GO TO the result is simply 5, but the sequence control provides a loop of instructions with the data starting at 8, and 3 being subtracted each time the computer goes through the sequence to give an output of 5, 2, −1, −4, −7, −10 etc. Even without knowing the details of program, it is quite easy to identify common computer processes that are using quite large loops. Payrolls, order forms and invoices all use the same set of instructions many times over.

A look at a special type of GO TO instruction will show what is actually behind the apparent ability of the computer to decide, check on something or wait for a special result. These instructions are different, as the central processor only acts on them under special circumstances, whereas the remainder of the time the instruction does nothing at all. An example of such an instruction is GO TO MIN 6 for GO TO ON FINDING MINUS VALUE TO 6. In long hand, the instruction would be written 'If the number in the central processor is a minus value then GO TO 6'. If the number is not minus, but 0 or positive, the GO TO 6 part will be ignored. By introducing GO TO MIN 6 as the third instruction in our subtraction program and using a self-explanatory instruction STOP, it is possible to illustrate a computer 'decision'.

1 LOAD 8
2 SUB 3
3 GO TO MIN 6
4 OUTPUT
5 GO TO 2
6 STOP

First time round the loop, the answer is 5. This is a plus value and so the GO TO MIN 6 will have no effect. Similarly, the second time round the loop the result is 2, still plus, and instruction 3 will again have no effect. The result after the third subtraction will be a $-1$ so instruction 3 will be followed, causing a skip to instruction 6. The result of following STOP will be to halt the central processor. Running this program could give the appearance of the computer deciding to take some special action, stopping, on some condition, a minus number. Such instructions are referred to as being conditional.

It is instructions like GO TO MIN that form the basis of all computer decisions. The use of these decisions can be seen easily in many computer systems. Conditional instructions would have to be used in a program to produce a special reminder note if a bank balance was minus, or to print WORK HARDER on a screen when a required operating speed is not being achieved. The point of considering software is to indicate how limited the basic functions of a computer actually are; their entire operation depends on following pre-determined instructions.

# 4
# Software

A program of instructions has to be drawn up before any micro-electronic processor can be used for a specific application. These programs, called software, are loaded into the microelectronic memory and executed by the processor at its own speed. In this chapter we look at the nature of software production, where it is done, who does it and how it has changed over the last thirty years.

## A crisis of productivity

In contrast to the production of the hardware on which programs run, the production of software is, at the moment, a process where capital has been unable to achieve a sustained initiative over labour. From management's point of view, a growing crisis of software productivity has been caused by an entrenched labour force which still uses craft practices.

On average, a programmer writing out instructions in a special computer language for a particular application will produce only ten to fifteen tested and workable instruction statements a day. Although a programmer may write hundreds of instructions every day, only this small handful will get through a rigorous testing process without significant amendment. The average salary for an experienced programmer in the UK in the late 1970s was about £4,250. Consequently, the cost of writing one program statement, which may only add two numbers together or pass control from one part of the program to another, was about £1.20. If we compare this cost of labour in software production with the total cost of the microelectronics on which the programs are run, we can see just how deep the productivity crisis is in software production.

The 64K bit random access memory was the hardware industry's standard in 1980. One chip of this density could store somewhere between 2,000 and 4,000 instructions. The chip costs about £2.85 but the cost of producing the tested software to load onto it would be anything between £2,400 and £4,800 in labour alone. It is clear from this single comparison that the productivity of software workers is far below that of hardware producers. Having bought the labour of programmers on the job markets of the major economies in the West, employers have failed to achieve the same level of productivity from this labour as they have achieved from labour in hardware production.

The high cost of software production is caused, management says, by the labour-intensive nature of the design and writing of programs. As we look at the production of software, and the composition of the labour force, we will see that the essential tasks in production are executed largely under the control of labour. As the chapter on hardware production shows, the essential tasks in the manufacture of the microelectronic devices are under the control of management and largely executed by capital's weapon in the class struggle – the machine.

*Conservative labour*

A leading computer consultant wrote recently in a guide to computers for company directors:

> Software costs are, in strong contrast to those of hardware, rising because the preparation of tailor-made software is essentially labour-intensive and, despite their keenness for other people to change their ideas, systems analysts and programmers are notoriously conservative in their own attitudes to fundamentally new and productive methods.

The composition of this conservative labour force, like their productivity, is in marked contrast to the profile of microelectronic production workers.

In the first place, the only international division of labour that does exist is among the metropolitan countries with the majority of software production done in the United States. The proportion of women in the labour force is also much lower in software; only 23% of programming jobs are filled by women and this proportion drops to 10% for the more powerful job of systems analysis and design. This low participation of women in software production was not always the case. All the programming on America's first computer was done by a group of women working for the Defence Department in the mid-1940s. The male electrical engineers who designed the Eniac computer realised only right at the end of the design that someone would have to write programs for it; it was considered a minor task so women were drafted in. But these women, mostly graduates in mathematics, soon showed that programming was a far from trivial task. Once this was realised by the men building proto-type computers in the late 1940s, the job of programming was taken over by men and the 'Eniac girls', as they were patronisingly dubbed, were the last group of women to have any significant control over computer programming.

Within the UK, the production of hardware is normally located in the areas worst hit by economic depression where wages have been forced down, unemployment is high and the state provides capital for new industrial development. But the concentration of software production, with a few exceptions, is focussed on the high wage areas of London and the South-East where 45% of all programmers and systems analysts work. The North, the North-East, East Anglia, Scotland and Wales between them have only 27% of all software producers.

The level of skill needed in the assembly of hardware has been so decomposed by the introduction of capital-intensive manufacturing methods that almost any labour force in any part of the world can be used. In contrast, the production of software still demands a high level of skill from the whole workforce and the pool of trained and experienced programmers now available is insufficient to produce the amount of software needed to turn the millions of microelectronic devices being produced into useful products. Programmers are therefore in a position to expect £500 to £1,000 extra a year before they will change to another job. A starting salary for a trainee pro-gammer in the late 1970s was about £3,000 a year; it rose with experience and averaged out to about £4,250. But 'good candidates who update their skills', as a contemporary salary report put it, could earn as much as £6,000.

## A new initiative

Managers are today trying to mount an initiative against this labour force to capture control of the production process and push down the average wage. Their methods are the ones that have already been successful over other workers: a further division of labour, an enforced separation of the worker and the product and the intro-duction of new labour organisations to replace individualised craft methods which currently dominate programming.

No one in hardware production, outside the small elite of designers, would conceive of the microelectronic device they were making as 'their chip'. Yet in software production the handicraft relationship between labour and its product exists to the point where ordinary programmers frequently do think and talk of the program they are working on as *their* program. This relationship reflects the control labour has over the production process and hence management's lack of control. It has therefore become a key focus in management's current initiative. Textbooks for managers in data processing clearly spell out that programmers 'must be made to understand' that what they are working on is a corporate asset, not their own property — they may make it, but they must understand that the software does not belong to them. A further division of labour within software production is being used as a tactic to achieve this objective.

A recent IBM publication aimed at managers of software departments outlined new methods of organisation which included the creation of a new job: the librarian.

> The librarian is responsible for picking up all computer output, good or bad, and filing it in the notebooks and archives of the development support library *where it becomes part of the public record*. By contrast, in traditional programming operations, the bad runs go into the waste basket, often destroying information of latent value, but certainly destroying information about errors of carelessness. The identification of all program data and computer runs as public assets, not private property, is a key principle in team operations.' (Emphasis added)

The product, and the labour that goes to make it, cannot, from management's point of view, remain the private property of labour — it must become the private property of the corporation. Output from the many unsuccessful attempts to get the program running is taken as 'positive proof of carelessness'. Unless the total working practice of software producers is out in the open, management will have little chance of controlling production.

There is, at the moment, a lot of discussion among managers over the best tactics to use in the current initiative. Lots of new methods are being proposed, but their central themes are much the same and the most popular solutions have so far been the introduction of librarians attached to teams of programmers.

The object of the team is to get a set of programmers working together, reviewing each other's work, while the librarian retrieves all the information about the labour process for management's scrutiny. The programmer will then be at a disadvantage in project and career reviews with management. The programmer can no longer appeal to a greater technical knowledge of software because the management will have documented proof of his or her errors of carelessness. Once again a product of labour will be used to confront labour as management tries to gain mastery of the production process.

This battle over control of the product goes hand in hand with attempts to quantify the process of software production in order to measure the performance of programmers against time and cost. The methods of software quantification available in the late 1970s were crude compared with the levels of quantification in hardware production or any other branch of engineering. But the leading US magazine for data processing managers held out the success of one company as an example to other managers. The senior management of a company with 14 data centres and nearly 1,000 software workers reported on a three-year project. Its aim was:

● To establish performance objectives.
● To record and report total performance.
● To provide the basis of comparison as a standard of comparing projects which would aid in determining future requirements and where costs should be reduced.
● To measure and compare performance of one programming project to another.
● To foster a competitive spirit that could be an incentive for improving performance.

The system that the company developed involved counting the lines of error-free code written by each programmer, measuring overtime, finding out exactly what labour was spent servicing various computer devices and measuring how fast programmers could fix errors in programs.

Even before the management began to tackle the bottlenecks which were revealed by the quantification process, the productivity of software workers in the company went up because their labour processes were under greater scrutiny. The number of mistakes in coding a line of instructions went down by 59%; the amount of later amendment required by each 1,000 lines of code dropped by 47% and the overtime worked by the 1,000 workers dropped by 56%. Summing up the project a senior manager said: 'As many functions as possible must be removed from the 'art' category of management. A measurement system is simply another tool which can be used by an alert management to increase productivity and quality, and then make the overall job of managing data processing easier.'

The initiative of senior management was successful in dragging the labour process of software production out into the open, out of the minds and closed relations of one programmer to another. The initiative rested on a computerised measurement system for which the programs were written by the software workers themselves. But it is not only the product of software labour that confronts software workers, hardware does as well.

## *Using productivity against software workers*

As the struggle over software production continues, management often uses the productivity it has extracted from hardware workers in attempts to outflank software workers. Management increasingly relies on trading off some of the speed and density of storage in microelectronics against the low productivity of software production. The most dramatic example of this was the development of high level programming languages nearly 20 years ago, a development which gave management only a little more control for a short time but a lot more productivity from each worker.

In January 1954 the first successful commercial application of a computer began in earnest when a computerised payroll for 1,700 workers at a Lyon's bakery in West London processed the weekly details and payslip for each worker in 1½ seconds. The system was developed on special hardware called Lyons Electronic Office (Leo). The design called for a close relationship between the hardware engineers and the programmers. The programmers had to know how the hardware worked before they could write the programs in a computer language which closely resembled the steps taken by the hardware. Programs had to be as compact as possible because there was so little storage in which to hold them during execution. Finally there were few aids to the testing and correcting of programs—when a program went wrong during tests, the entire contents of the computer store had to be printed out as a long string of numbers with very little guidance to show which number represented an instruction a letter or a numeric value. The programmers had power over the process of producing the programs and this ensured that they received a high status and salary. They were all men.

Manufacturers of computer hardware realised in the mid-1950s that the scientific and technical markets they had relied on for the last eight years were not as large or profitable as clerical applications such as the Leo system. But these new markets could not be tapped if the new applications took as much time and skill to develop as was demanded by the low level of programming language then available. Unless the bottleneck of the skilled programmer with an intimate knowledge of the hardware was broken, the growth of the market, and future applications would be limited. A movement therefore began among some of the biggest users and manufacturers under the co-ordination of the US Department of Defence, to develop new languages in which applications could be written faster. One of the explicit aims of the project was to get a programming language that managers could use themselves with a minimum of time and effort. Under the guidance of the Department of Defence, the language designers came up with a specification for the Common Business Oriented Language (Cobol).

Manufacturers initially resisted the pressure to develop intermediate software which would take statements in Cobol and compile them into instructions that their hardware could execute, principally because of the large investment needed. But their resistance was overcome when the Navy Department made it a condition of future sales of computers that they should have such a compiler. The initial attempts to write these compilers were not, in the main, successful. Software workers tried to design compilers which would produce code that was as compact and as efficient in its use of the hardware as the code which would be written in a low-level language by an experienced programmer. Only when this objective was ditched, around 1963, did Cobol compilers that worked begin to come onto the market. By now the hardware was based not on valves but on transistors and the much faster, more compact hardware could be used to compensate for very inefficient code written in a high level language like Cobol. It was soon discovered that programmers wrote the same number of reliable statements, whatever language they were writing code in. As each Cobol statement had the same processing power as a number of low-level statements, its introduction achieved an absolute increase in productivity. But at the same time there was a change in the composition of the workforce.

## A new workforce

The boom in computer applications for commercial systems took off in the early 1960s on the basis of this increased productivity. The amount of programming that had to be done rose enormously and thousands of new jobs were created for programmers in the growing data-processing departments set up by users. The new computer applications had to be designed before they were written and, alongside the introduction of a whole new workforce, a division of labour was introduced between the job of designing the programs and actually writing the statements to run on the hardware. The new job of systems analyst attracted recruits from the organisation and methods departments who had already been investigating and adapting methods of clerical work for the past 20 years. It also attracted many of the older, skilled programmers, especially those who saw it as a way of avoiding the management aspects of running data-processing departments. Finally, the manufacturers found that they needed the skills of a growing number of programmers to write both the new compilers and the other forms of more sophisticated software necessary for their hardware to execute a Cobol program.

Some of the programmers who were skilled in the craft of writing compact and fast-running programs in low-level codes stayed to fight out what they conceived of as a technical battle. Their code used the physical resources of the computer more efficiently but their arguments fell on deaf ears. Management was not looking for efficiency from the machine but from the labour process of software production.

Thus in the brief period from about 1957 to 1964, management took an initiative against labour which, in the short term, proved successful and laid the basis for the massive growth of computer systems in the next two decades.

### Rebuilding software skills

Managers did not write their own programs in Cobol as was originally conceived; they were too busy managing the phenomenal growth of data processing departments in this period. Instead, thousands of people who had never seen a computer, many of them without university degrees, were quickly trained in Cobol programming and thrown into the job of writing applications. With managers distracted by growth, the new workforce was able to rebuild a new set of skills to tackle the new type of programming because they held a powerful position in the production process. Their labour was precious at a time when managers were frantically looking for new recruits to staff their programming departments. The development of these skills was essential if the new applications were to be completed so that payrolls, stock controls, invoicing and production monitoring could be computerised. But the price management paid for this growth was a decreasing amount of control over the labour process it had just restructured. The very practices of programming were privatised, almost remystified, as far as management was concerned.

With each new development in hardware, from the introduction of the transistor onwards, there was a corresponding development in software which increased the productivity of software production. In some minor ways management clawed back some of the control it had lost but in the main productivity was increased only by giving programmers more powerful tools. After integrated circuits were introduced in computer hardware around 1964 this new level of hardware productivity was used to introduce more complex software which, this time, took some of the routine tasks of keeping the computer running out of the hands of the programmer. Operating systems, which co-ordinate the running of a number of programs at the same time, were developed once hardware was fast, compact and cheap enough to execute more than one program at a time. The introduction of operating systems attacked the skills needed by computer operators, reducing them to the role of machine minders from a position where they had minute by minute control over the computer.

When hundreds of transistors were put on a single microelectronic device with medium scale integration from the early 1970s, database management systems and teleprocessing monitors began to be introduced. With a database management system running on the computer, programmers no longer need to know where within a computer any data is stored. Instead of having to maintain and access a lot of individual files of information, programmers concentrating on the application need only write a single statement instructing the database management system to get data and present it in the right form. The new productivity gained in hardware also meant that computer terminals remote from the central computer site could access the centrally held data and programs over telecommunication lines. Instead of writing the software to drive these telecommunication networks, a teleprocessing monitor program is supplied by the manufacturer.

These new, more complex pieces of software which control a computer system are either supplied by the hardware manufacturer or by independent software houses. Providing these more complex software products has embroiled software houses and manufacturers in the increasingly important tasks of producing large quantities of reliable, predictable and cheap software themselves.

### The myth of software engineering

But software suppliers, like the managers in users' data processing departments, are having an increasingly difficult time doing this with current methods of software production. The UK computer company ICL, for instance, launched a new range of computers in the mid-1970s but, even by the end of the decade, the operating systems designed for these computers were far from reliable. And

IBM had to publicly postpone, for the first time in its history, delivery of a new small-business computer by over six months because the database system that came with it was not working to specification. When it did announce the new shipment dates, IBM also increased the storage size of the computers—a clear example of trading the inefficiency software against the efficiency of hardware.

This crisis of software production is expressed academically in a debate over the best methods to solve the technical problems of constructing large and reliable software. In the design and programming of large software projects like the development of a new database system or a compiler, there are hardly any universal tools which can be used. When, for instance, a team of designers and programmers was established within ICL in the late 1960s to write an operating system the first thing they had to do was to write, test and get running a special programming language of their own in which to write the operating system. Having done this they had to write more software to monitor the performance of the computer as it tested the operating system because, again, no universal tool existed. Finally, they had to design another set of programs to help them conduct a *post mortem* on the computer when the operating system failed tests.

In other engineering prodjects the basic tools for the design, development, monitoring and diagnosis are already at hand. They may need some amendment but they would not have to be built from scratch; it is rather like having to make a saw every time you wanted to cut a piece of wood. On top of this lack of tools, there is no generally accepted way of talking and thinking about large pieces of software without getting bogged down in the particular details of each application. The lack of all these tools shows that software production is still very much at the craft stage and that management has failed to break with labour's control of the processes of production.

# 5
# Desk-top Models:
# Microprocessors in the Office

*Introduction*

A few years ago, the electrical manufacturer Philips estimated that, exclusive of author's time, a letter costs £4 to produce. In 1978, *The Guardian* pointed out that, whereas a typist with a certificate proving that she can type 50 words per minute should, theoretically, be able to type 1,750 lines of text a day, the average copy-typist produces only about 250 lines a day. High cost and low productivity characterise office work. With clerical and administrative workers making up 30% of all workers in manufacturing and 45% of the total UK workforce, it is apparent that within the current economic crisis, the office, its inhabitants, and traditional office organisation are a bottleneck in the process of capital accumulation in private and nationalised industries. With public expenditure cuts, the office is one of the main areas for rationalisation, and hence, cost-cutting in the public sector.

*High cost, low productivity*

There have been three major periods of growth in office work. The initial introduction of women into offices and the subsequent feminisation of office work during the last quarter of the nineteenth century resulted not just from the introduction of machinery, notably the typewriter, but crucially from the expansion of trade and commerce at the height of British imperialism. Secondly, the growing demand for clerical workers was further enhanced by changes in the organisation of work in production processes during the 1920s. These changes arose from the widespread application of Taylorist techniques to manufacturing which relied upon employers' acquisition of knowledge about all the human actions within the labour process in manufacturing. Only with this knowledge can machinery be designed to pace or replace these human motions as part of the attempt to gain greater control over the labour process and increase profit levels. As Taylor said of scientific management:

> It is aimed at establishing a clear cut and novel division of mental and manual labour through the workshops. It is based upon the precise time and motion study of each worker's job in isolation, and relegates the entire mental part of the task in hand to the management staff. (*Shop Management*, 1903)

Capital's demand for knowledge and hence control has resulted in increasing numbers of workers being involved in the acquisition, storage, transformation and presentation of this information on behalf of capital, with a declining proportion involved at the actual point of production.

A third major period of growth can be attributed to the post-war boom. There was a massive expansion in whole new sectors of industry, particularly in consumer durables and light engineering, parallel with an increasing concentration of capital through take-overs and mergers, in manufacturing, banking and finance. Banking and finance grew as more people took out insurance policies, and bank accounts were opened as wages and salaries were paid through banks. The Building Societies grew wtih the expansion of home ownership. The 1944 Education Act reduced illiteracy and opened up opportunities for working class people to increase their chances of upward social mobility by moving into the white collar sector. Perhaps most important, however, was the inception of the welfare state which became a major white collar employer in hospitals, social security, local government and education.

Until now, office managements have relied on informal methods of personnel organisation and control. These methods are highly personalised and rooted both in the traditional relations of male domination and female subordination, and in concerns with status and prestige springing from the division between manual and intellectual labour.

Such organisational methods embody several inefficiencies which effectively undermine profitability. On the one hand they enable women office workers to engage in non-working activities during working hours by organising their working lives around the sexual division of labour to create time and space for themselves in a way which clearly challenges managerial control. The control methods applied to women office workers are not based on strict disciplinary and economic constraints, but on personalised, patriarchal attitudes. Women are controlled by flattery and praise and encouraged to develop a sense of loyalty to individual bosses or departments, and hence towards the company or organisation. These patriarchal attitudes, however, enable them to create informal work cultures within which they establish working patterns which cannot be penetrated by masculine work standards and allow them to engage in activities which cannot easily be controlled. While these activities—such as conversations about the family, boyfriends, fashion and general domestic concerns—reinforce and reproduce their oppression as women, they can clearly be seen as resistance to the alienation and boredom of office work. There is, in most offices, a tendency for managements to turn a blind eye to such time wasting activities, for much as managers may dislike them, they do recognise they are likely to get more out of their women office workers if they treat them reasonably and respect their concerns.

The other side of the patriarchal form of control, is the tendency of top managements to incorporate the loyalty of their lower orders through overt status symbols, most notably, by providing them with secretaries. For many managers it is not just the company car, but also the acquisition of a secretary which proves that they have made it. But at the same time, it must be recognised that giving a manager his own secretary is rarely an indication of his increased workload— few bosses generate sufficient work to keep a secretary busy for eight hours a day. This is despite the general tendency to load the secretary down with domestic work, like making tea and coffee, watering plants, keeping the office tidy and even buying birthday cards for his family.

These traditional patterns of control, rooted as they are in patriarchal notions of femininity, are being challenged by ideas coming from the women's movement. This challenge has been, surprisingly, recognised by the joint managing director of Olivetti, Franco de Benedetti. At a London conference in March 1979 on the 'Impact of Electronic Technology in the Office', de Benedetti discussed one of the forces which could 'oppose and hinder the diffusion of office automation'. The relationship between the executive and his secretary is characterised by psychological factors; it is, he said, 'loaded with meanings and values which extend far beyond the purely working relationship, and virtually becomes a set of "private relationships".' He then goes on to note that 'given the high percentage of female personnel employed in the unstructured sector of office work, it should be remembered that this psychological reality is being profondly (sic) changed by feminism'. Indeed, in recent years there has been a clear upsurge in criticism by women office workers of the types of subservient, domestic tasks they are expected to undertake which are in addition to the tasks they are actually being paid for.

At another level, where informal personalised forms of control have been broken down as a result of increasing bureaucratisation, such as in the public sector, there has been an increase in trade union membership among women office workers—a direct threat to the traditional forms of managerial control. Although trades unionism does not directly challenge patriarchy itself, it can mean that in areas such as wage demands, managerial control can be undermined. In non-unionised offices, without the advantages of collective bargaining, women have to make their wage demands individually to a man. For many women this can be an extremely embarassing situation which requires that they have to admit to a man with whom they have a personal, yet professional relationship, that they cannot afford to live on their wages. It is a situation which many would prefer to avoid, even though it then means continuing to exist on a low wage. The alternative chosen by many women is to change jobs to increase their wage and this accounts in large part, for the high turnover of office staff. Of course, women with children who find work locally to fit in with childcare arrangements have no such freedom to change jobs.

*Figure 5.1*: Typing cost relative to total office labour cost

Total: $3.54 billion

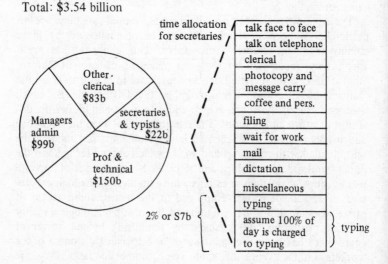

With the aid of word processor manufacturers and consultants, managements are becoming increasingly aware of the inefficiencies of their traditional methods of organisation. The above diagram, which is part of the word processor sales techniques employed by consultants, clearly demonstrates how much of a secretary's typical working day is actually spent typing—2%. While this is not true for typists, this is the basis on which word processors are being sold. Word processors are designed to cut out that part of the working day which is spent on time-wasting, non-typing duties such as photocopying, dictation and filing. They are also designed to subordinate the worker to the machine and to develop more formal forms of control than those we have described. In conjunction with developments such as electronic mail and facsimile transmission, the word processor aids deskilling and hence the cheapening of office labour and offers management the means by which they can increase their control over the office work process.

## The automated office

Two factors have inhibited the complete rationalisation of office work. Firstly, within an environment which has functioned through personalised control, there has been a refusal at all levels of management to even recognise a need for change. Inefficiency may be recognised and from time to time measures may be taken to reduce waste and tighten up organisational procedures, but historically there has existed among most office workers a sense of familiarity with well tried and tested methods of organisation which are comfortable and relaxed. This conservatism is still one of the major obstacles to change. Secondly, the physical equipment by which office work could be completely reorganised has, until now, not been available. It was only when semiconductor engineers discovered that they could process words as well as data electronically, that the word processor industry took off.

Historically, increased profitability has been achieved by managements increasing their control over the labour process and lowering the cost at which they have to purchase labour by breaking up workers' organisation and by rendering individuals' skills redundant—the process of deskilling.

A word processor consists of a typewriter keyboard linked to a computer which enables information to be stored and retrieved. Information is keyed into the machine and displayed on the visual display unit (VDU), and only when the operator has checked that it is correct by reading the screen is anything printed. The word processor's more salient selling points are that it can store, say, the skeleton paragraphs of standard letters, which can be recalled by keying in a reference number to display it on the VDU. The details are then keyed in by the operator and the whole document may be printed out on a separate machine at speeds of up to 2,000 lines a minute. This eliminates costly re-typing and can be applied to a whole range of typical office material such as standard letters, reports, manuscripts and address lists. Since word processors have editing facilities, instead of completely re-typing drafts in their entirety, changes can be made simply by deleting or adding words, sentences or paragraphs.

In all, the word processor reduces the time that is necessary to produce a document by eliminating re-typing and, as the manufacturers proudly say, it also reduces the labour that is needed— work that previously required three typists can now be done by one word processor operator.

To understand how the word processor deskills office workers and also increases managerial control, we must look at other features of the equipment and the way it is being introduced.

Women operators test word processors at the end of the biggest word processor production line in Europe at Olivetti's Italian plant.

*Deskilling*

Typing is a skill which requires some years to perfect. The typical Royal Society of Arts typing examination requires an ability to perform certain skills such as centering headings, tabulation, setting out documents neatly, as well as the attainment of high speeds. These functions can be carried out automatically by the word processor at the touch of a button. The ability to type both fast and accurately becomes less important. All that is required is a familiarity with the keyboard. If the operator makes an error—and at this point she is not typing onto paper but onto the screen—she simply backspaces and types the correct word or letter and the error disappears. As a result typing as a skill becomes redundant but perhaps more important is the other aspect of deskilling, the loss of control over the job.

The degree to which one can assess an individual worker's skill depends to a great extent on the amount of control s/he has over the job. With traditional typing, the amount of control in the hands of the individual typist depends upon her position within the hierarchy of secretarial work, but we make certain generalisations on the understanding that not every typist or secretarial worker is in a one-to-one personal or private situation. Even the typist in the typing pool has some measure of control over, for instance, when she puts the paper into the machine, how she sets out her work, where she sets the margins, whether the salutation is four or five lines down from the name and address of the recipient. Such features may appear unimportant to the outsider, but in an environment which depends to a large extent on control through flattery, praise and the engendering of a feeling of indispensability an inevitable consequence is the need to feel one is an *individual* and not just a cog in a well oiled machine. It is, therefore, common for women to develop filing systems that only they can understand, not just in order to make themselves indispensable, but to bring some degree of individuality to their work.

With the aid of word processor manufacturers and consultants, managements are beginning to recognise that a crucial move in developing more efficient office organisations and typing systems is to depersonalise the relationship between bosses and secretaries. The word processing centre (WPC) is created to offer an overall typing service as part of the attempt to break down that costly individual relationship, and the individual typist is no longer permitted to reference typed documents with her own initials—a common practice is to use the author's reference then WPC/job number instead. The assumption underlying this is that the author should not know who has keyboarded his or her particular document, so any questions s/he has about it should be addressed to the supervisor, leaving the operators free from interruptions and free from the opportunity for idle chatter, free to complete the only task they are being paid for—keyboarding.

## Fragmentation

The introduction of word processors rests on an extension of an existing division of labour. All firms and organisations are divided into separate departments; within departments individuals are engaged on individual aspects of a job. For example, an invoice will be made up by one person, checked by another and typed by a third, and the postal department will take care of despatching it. Just as the whole manufacturing process is based on the separation of conception from execution, there are divisions within mental labour itself in which women occupy the lower rungs. While there has been a tendency historically for the secretarial worker's job to develop as a completely manual function, many secretarial workers find they have auxiliary tasks to perform, such as filing, the responsibility for an individual's mail and making coffee. The object of word processing systems is to further fragment the secretarial job. High levels of efficiency and cost effectiveness are best achieved by stripping away all possible distractions from the actual job of typing.

## Control – or lack of it

Some managements may develop more philanthropic systems allowing the authors to consult directly with the operators, or allowing the operators to move on a rota system from the word processor to an ordinary electric typewriter, thus meeting agreements reached on health and safety about eye strain for VDU operators. Most installations, however, are designed to give one person, the supervisor, all the responsibility for ensuring that work is carried out to certain standards, and for maintaining a high degree of output. The individual operators have no control over layout and are expected to keyboard continuously. In those organisations that have abolished the use of shorthand as time wasting and cost ineffective, audio systems have been introduced that allow dictation to be fed automatically to the operator as soon as her station is freed. These 'endless loop' systems function by having an exact record of how *fast* each operator can keyboard and how much work she still has to complete—with this knowledge, the system then allocates new dictation work to whichever operator can complete it within a given period, storing it until she is free. Operators are, therefore, continuously plugged in with no idea of how much more work they have to do, when it will stop, and when they can maybe sneak a break.

Even without an endless loop system, the operator's productivity can be monitored. The word processor's memory logs exactly how much work she is producing and rewards or warnings can be given accordingly. This, perhaps more than the straightforward fragmentation and deskilling of typing, amounts to the most effective way in which managements can exert their control.

Proponents of word processing argue that the new technology will lighten the burden of office work and free secretarial workers for more interesting work. Perhaps the top secretaries will be given a more administrative function, but the largely working-class women who are on the lower levels of the hierarchy will find their work becoming more boring, routine and intensified.

In the USA where office automation and word processors are more common than in this country, the number of lower-skilled machine operating jobs have increased, widening the gap between top jobs performed by white women and the low-level, low-paid jobs performed largely by black women. As one book on American office workers describes it:

> Racism is . . . clearly visible to anyone who walks through a big office company. Pretty young white women work as private secretaries in the carpeted offices of the new downtown buildings. Black clericals are mainly reserved for the keypunch room, the typing pool, or the data processing centre across town—the routine, pressurised, low-paid jobs. (Jean Tepperman, *Servants Not Machines: Office Workers Speak Out*, Beacon Press, Boston, USA, 1978, p. 49.)

As word processors increase the polarisation between top secretarial, administrative jobs on the one hand and routine machine minding jobs on the other, it is apparent, especially in local-government offices like the Greater London Council, that not only white, working-class women, but also black women will have their promotion prospects hampered by being stuck at the bottom of the hierarchy. In fact, even in the traditional office, black and white working-class women are likely to stay in low level jobs as promotion is blocked to them by virtue of their class and colour. The impact of word processors will be not to supplement existing limitations, but to make them more apparent. A more useful way of illustrating the impact of word processors on individual workers is to allow one to speak for herself. Carole worked for five years as a word processor operator in the world's largest bank in San Francisco.

'Secretarial people didn't like the word processors because they already had the skills and the pay, but it was a novelty. You know, everybody was excited to learn this new thing that was going to help alleviate boredom and make life easier and then they found out that they really didn't do that at all—in fact they made it more boring.'

*'Can you say why they made it more boring?'*

'Because people felt that they were plugged into machines, that they were appendages to machines rather than people performing functions with other people.'

*'Is that true for the clerical and the secretarial workers?'*

'Yes, very much so. We used to have jokes about how we expected that soon they'd chain us to our desks and give us catheters, so we'd never have to go to the bathroom. And the thing is that once word processing or video display equipment is introduced, it's possible to keep track exactly of the amount of productivity each individual displays and set rises and evaluations accordingly. And people feel very pressurised to get their production out. The standards are raised. When I first started at the bank, the standards were 8,000 keystrokes an hour and when I left they were 12,000 over a five-year time period.'

# 6
# Small Batch

Small batch methods of production are used in almost every part of the mechanical engineering industry as well as many parts of the instrument engineering and electrical engineering industries. The products of small batch engineering are machines, or parts of machines, and so they enter into the production of every other item in the economy. Consequently, any productivity increase in small batch machine-making can, over time, affect the rest of the economy. In the nineteenth century, it was recognised that the increase in overall social productiveness signalled by the Industrial Revolution was limited by the way machinery was produced with hand tools by very skilled, craft metal workers. The mechanisation of machine-making was the major technical advance in production of the late nineteenth century. It seems that, based on developments in microelectronics, the late twentieth century will see further attempts to drastically cheapen machine-making through the application of microelectronic technology to small batch engineering production.

## What is small batch production?

In mass production, the output is a continuous stream of standardised products. The product is standardised to go with a standardised production process. This entails the use of special purpose machinery, operated by semi-skilled or unskilled workers, organised on a flow-line principle whereby machines are arranged in a set sequence through which each component passes. The whole sequence may even be completely mechanised so that it is automatic.

In small batch production the output is a wide variety of items, a large proportion of which are made directly to the stated requirements of the customers, who are usually other firms. The output is therefore of high variety, and it meets a fluctuating and unpredictable demand. Of machined components made in Britain, 40% are produced in batches of less than 50 items, and they are worth £12,000 million (1980 prices).

*Figure 6.1*: Labour involved and tasks in a small batch engineering factc

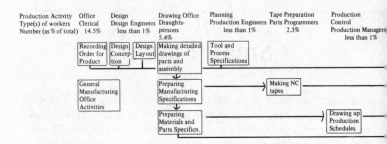

*Sources*: Based on R. M. Bell, *Changing Technology and Manpower Req*
Economic Development Office, *Machine tools: the employees' view of*

The high variety in small batch production means that succeeding batches require different machining operations in different sequences. Even the assembly of components cannot be organised around flowline methods, since the final product (say, a machine tool) can be as variable as its components. To provide the flexibility that the products demand, conventional small batch production systems consist of general purpose machinery, craft labour, and what is known as the functional layout of machinery (for example all the lathes are located in one part of the factory).

Figure 6.1 depicts the labour involved in a small batch factory that makes machine tools. The figure gives the approximate percentage of workers in each step of the production process and describes what tasks each group of workers perform. Altogether about 55% of the workforce is involved in shop floor production activities and 35% is in design, technical and clerical jobs. The remaining 10% is in various ancillary activities.

Over the last twenty years the proportion of shopfloor workers has declined compared to that of administrative, technical and clerical workers, though only slightly. And although a majority (60-70%) of the shop floor workers are still defined as craftsmen, (they are overwhelmingly men) their number has declined both relatively and absolutely whereas semi-skilled and unskilled workers (defined in official statistics as other production workers) have increased.

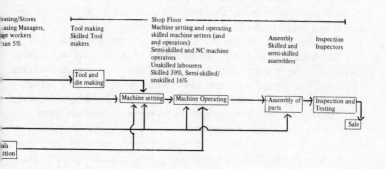

*s in the Engineering Industry,* (London, 1972) and National *stry* (London, 1977).

## Management's struggle for control

Despite the increasing number of white-collar workers and semi-skilled machine operators and assemblers, small batch engineering is still a bastion of craft metalworkers. Such workers, who interpret drawings, set up machines, monitor the machines' performance and even plan the order of the jobs to be done, clearly have considerable control over the tasks they carry out. Their strategic position in this type of production, exemplified in their strong trade union organisation, has been consistently attacked by managements over the last hundred years in an attempt to reduce this control and so make small batch production more 'rational', more predictable and more plannable. Towards that end new machinery has been introduced. New techniques of organisation, such as scientific management, have been implemented. New forms of the division of labour have been installed, like the creation of more levels of management or the introduction of technicians. All of these have been the occasion of struggles over exactly how the proposed changes should be implemented, so that management has not always realised the benefits that it had hoped for. Workers have constantly sought and often found ways round new forms of discipline.

It has been estimated that parts produced by conventional small batch production methods may cost between 10 and 30 times more than they would if they were mass produced. This is principally because the machines have to be reset between each batch, so that only a small proportion of a machine's life—usually no greater than one hour in five—is spent in actual operation. There are also considerable hold-ups in the movement of components from one functional area to another, so that a component may spend as much as 99% of its time on the shopfloor queuing between machines. In a small batch engineering factory, then, a number of batches of different items will be being made at one time—some actually being machined by skilled workers, some being moved around the shop from one group of machines to another by unskilled labourers, some just waiting for the next operation to be performed on them, and some being assembled or inspected.

The final product can be cheapened by introducing into these production methods any changes that reduce the delays and stocks of work in progress; that make easier the complex process of organising the most efficient flows of all the batches from design to assembly, or that reduce the amount of highly-paid skilled labour that is required for designing and drawing, for operating and setting the machines or for planning the production process. In small batch production, microelectronics offers managements new solutions to their organisational problems of a kind that are potentially more extensive than any they have tried before.

## Applications of microelectronics to small batch production

Microelectronic-based machines and equipment can be applied to small batch production in five ways—in the product itself, in design and drawing, in machining, in assembly, and in production control. (A sixth could be added, if we considered new office technologies.) The potential of microelectronics is such that the various aspects of small batch production could be brought together in a total system, with the workers' place in it much more rigorously defined and controlled than now. In short, microelectronics offers capital the *possibility* of turning small batch engineering production into an integrated process industry.

## 1. Products

The advent of any versatile new technology can often lead to products that are copies of existing ones but that are produced more cheaply by completely different processes (compare injection moulded or heat-formed plastic toys with their machined, assembled, metal or wooden equivalents). Such is, potentially, the case with new machinery which, by using microelectronic components, will require far fewer parts than electro-mechanical systems. This has clear implications for the number of workers required to make the components. However, the full potential of using micro-electronics in this way, in smaller, more powerful machine-control systems, will take some time to be realised. A lot of product re-design will first be necessary.

## 2. Design and drawing

The last 15 years have seen the increasing use of computer-aided automatic devices in this aspect of small batch production. Electronic calculators and computers are routinely used by design engineers for the complex numerical calculations involved in the actual design of a component or machine. In addition, however, there are now machines that can rapidly convert these numerical calculations into an actual drawing, either on paper or a video screen, with only limited assistance (if any) from draughtspersons. This is Computer-Aided Design (CAD). Some of the most advanced CAD systems can go further than just producing drawings; they can also draw up manufacturing specifications and even prepare tapes for numerically controlled machine tools.

At the moment, CAD equipment is not much used in small batch production. The equipment is concentrated in a few industries, namely, electronics, where it is used in the design of chips them-selves; in aerospace and chemical plant construction; and it is beginning to be introduced into automobile, ship and heavy elec-trical equipment design. However, microelectronics, by making the computer part of CAD devices cheaper and more powerful, increases the range of design and drawing activities that can be done by machines. Further, the machine integration of designing, drawing and preparing specifications for manufacture proper becomes techni-cally feasible. The prospect of cheaper CAD systems makes it likely that small batch engineering firms will begin to install them over the next ten years. The role of labour in such integrated systems would clearly be considerably different to that in design and drawing now. The number of people required for drawing and preparing manu-facturing instructions would be drastically reduced, though the effects on those involved in creative design would not be so dramatic.

## 3. Machining

There are a limited set of machining operations that are performed in small batch production since turning, milling and drilling take up well over 90% of the total machining time. The history of such machines has been one of inventions that increase the speed, accuracy and repeatability of operations while reducing the craft labour that is required. From the late 1940s, this has meant the slow, but increasing, introduction of numerically-controlled (NC) machine tools. These can offer a variety of tools to a metal piece, that cut, drill and grind in sequence according to the specifications that are coded in some control device, commonly a paper tape. Since a different paper tape will produce a different sequence of tool movements, NC machines are 'more flexible than conventional ones and require only one set-up (the making of the tape) for one type of component.

Even though there is no technical requirement for the different tasks necessary to operate NC machines to be allocated to separate workers, there has been a tendency to separate out the tasks of conception and execution. Table 6.1 compares the number of hours needed to set up and operate a conventional machine and an NC machine carrying out the same task, in this case, machining a batch of castings. The first three lines refer to the first set-up of the machines; the second three are concerned with repeating the machining process, after the initial set-up. As the table shows, for NC machines the tapes will be prepared from drawings, by technical workers — the parts programmers — while the machines will actually be operated by semi-skilled (non-craft) labour. The organising and machine-setting skills of the craft metalworkers are no longer required. Although more conceptual labour (measured in hours worked) is required than for conventional machines, the total number of hours required is less.

It should be pointed out that the table compares the amounts of different types of labour required by individual machines. The high cost of NC machines means that they will only account for a fraction of all the machines in a typical small batch engineering factory. At present the reduction in the need for skilled machine setters and operators in a factory or industry as a whole has not been as great as the figures in the table might suggest. But the situation will change rapidly. In 1976 there were about 10,000 NC machines out of a total of 900,000 machine tools in the UK, about half of them in the mechanical engineering sector. It has been suggested that by the 1990s there will be between 23,000 and 40,000 NC machines in the UK.

*Table 6.1:* Workhours required to operate a conventional machine and an NC machine for batch production of castings.

| | Conventional Machines | | | NC Machines | | |
|---|---|---|---|---|---|---|
| | Types of workers | Hours worked | % of total | Types of workers | Hours worked | % of total |
| **For first specifications:** | | | | | | |
| Conception | Supervisors Inspectors Tool/Fixture designers | 2060 | 22 | Process engineer Supervisors Inspectors Parts programmers Tool/Fixture designers | 2556 | 65 |
| Execution | Skilled Metalworkers (craftworkers) | 6872 | 75 | NC tool setters | 412 | 10 |
| | Unskilled benchhands | 268 | 3 | NC operators | 965 | 25 |
| | | 9200 | | | 3933 | |
| **For repeat specifications:** | | | | | | |
| Conception | as above | 1950 | 21 | as above except for process engineer | 860 | 38 |
| Execution | Craftworkers | 6872 | 76 | NC tool setters | 412 | 19 |
| | unskilled | 268 | 3 | NC operators | 965 | 43 |
| | | 9090 | | | 2237 | |

*Source:* adapted from R. M. Bell, *Changing Technology and Manpower Requirements in the Engineering industry*, (London, 1972).

## Direct Numerical Control

The introduction of NC machines may reduce the degree of direct control over work scheduling and over machine operation exercised by the shop-floor metalworker but it cannot eliminate it. Workers can slow down the speed of the machine by using the override switch which is intended for cutting out the tape control if something seems to be going wrong with the machine. NC technology, making use of cheaper, smaller and more powerful electronic control systems rather than tapes, is being developed in part to combat the resistance that workers have shown to the last generation of NC-technology. (H. Shaiken, *Radical America*, November-December 1979).

This is the case with Direct Numerical Control (DNC) of machine tools, in which a group of machine tools are linked to a mini-computer. Figure 6.2 illustrates a Japanese DNC system of the early 1970s. However, such machines are as yet not very widespread; approximately 100 are in use in the USA making airframe parts, tractor parts and axles, and 80 in Japan, making railway engines and tractor parts. In Britain there are only a few pilot installations.

Some DNC systems are associated with fully mechanised loading and unloading, sometimes using robots. (The example in Figure 6.2 is only partially mechanised.) With the addition of 'automatic work-piece transport' systems DNC machines are usually called Flexible Manufacturing Systems.

## Factories without workers?

However, even the flexible manufacturing systems fall short of the potential that is predicted for microelectronic-based, computer-controlled systems. These are known as Automated Small Batch Production Systems (ASPs). In the mid-1970s a committee was set up in Britain to investigate what ASPs would look like and what the government could do to stimulate innovation in small batch production. It consisted of engineers and managers from the National Engineering Laboratory and a number of large British engineering companies: Vickers, BOC, Kearney & Trecker Marwin, Plessey, Rolls Royce and GEC. Other firms such as ICL, Plessey and Ferranti, and academics gave considerable assistance.

In its report, *Automated Small Batch Production* (National Engineering Laboratory, Glasgow, 1978) the committee said that an ASP system should 'completely remove workers from the arduous side of production (tempo, noise, heat, fumes, danger, monotony) and raise them to the status of planners, controllers or supervisors –

*Figure 6.2*: Direct computer control system (used in rolling stock repair–maintenance shop of Japanese National Railways). 'Fujitsu Fanuc' System-K.

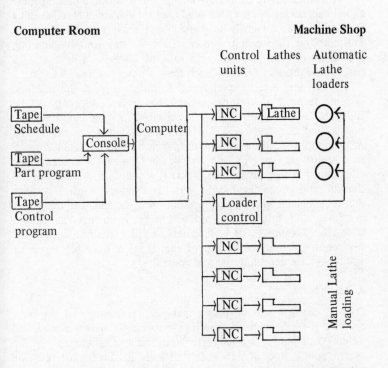

Four operators work the Seven n–c lathes (equivalent to 20 operators on 20 conventional lathes).

*Source*: R. M. Bell, *Changing Technology and Technical Requirements in the Engineering Industry*, (London, 1972).

analogous to the development of the chemical industry'. The committee hopes that by 1990 a system will have been proved that consists of at least 8 linked NC machines with a direct labour force of no more than 21 and with productivity on each machine three to seven times greater than on present machines.

Such productivity gains have already been achieved in a Japanese experimental factory, the Methodology for Unmanned Metalworking factory, a project heavily supported by the Japanese Government. This employs 10 people to produce components normally requiring, it is claimed, 700. It produces a total of 30 items a day out of a range of 50 product types in batch sizes of anything from 9 to 25.

Though this is an experimental factory, many of the machine systems techniques and procedures that it is developing will be applicable to many other factories engaged in small batch production throughout the world. Certainly the system proposed by the ASP Committee is of a size and output that could be installed by up to 500 British firms by the end of the century with significant effects on the amount of labour that is required. It is clear that the cheaper and more technically versatile machine control systems that microelectronics make possible will extend the range of machines that small batch production managements can choose from. But because of its high variety, small batch production will still require, to the annoyance of capital, a considerable degree of worker involvement, initative and control.

## 4. Assembly

Product changes will obviously make easier assembly of the final product of small batch engineering. In particular, new techniques of welding and joining are likely to be introduced. These include the use of robots and of new materials such as super adhesives. For example, Kawasaki is developing automatic assembly of an agricultural petrol engine, using robots; however, so far only part of the assembly process has become automated. Robots are not yet sophisticated enough, not so much in their computing abilities, but in sensing and operating. So robot assembly is not very near for small batch production – the final products are too complex and too variable for the robots of the 1980s.

## 5. Production control

The advent of cheaper, more sophisticated computers has considerable implications for the control of production systems as complex as those involved in making small batches. Computers can be used not just to enable direct control of machine tool operations (as in DNC) but also for automatic inspection, stock control, keeping a track of partly-finished components, calculating machine loadings and analysing how much labour is used. In short, computers can rapidly carry out the complex calculations needed to maximise output and minimise costs and production times, taking into account machining and queuing times, the costs and availability of raw materials, and the labour storage space necessary for the components that are being produced in the shop at a particular time. The use of computers to draw up production schedules in this way is called Computer Aided Manufacture (CAM).

CAM fits together with both Computer Aided Design and the computer-aided machining systems already described. In fact it is not possible to conceive of a factory without workers unless all the aspects of small batch production — design, drawing production planning, machining, assembly and inspection — are integrated into a new system of computer-aided production. It is conceivable that full computer-aided production systems will be commonplace in small batch engineering production in the next century, but cost and development problems will limit their application before that to the largest firms making the simplest range of products.

## Effects on employment

In the UK 900,000 people work in mechanical engineering. Another 900,000 work in instrument or electrical engineering and 500,000 produce other metal goods and many of these use small batch production methods. The new machines and organisational techniques described above will obviously have a significant effect on these employment levels. J. Remmerswaal forecasts that by the mid-1990s automation of the information flow (as he calls CAD/CAM) and general rationalisation will increase productivity by 200-300% in small batch production (summarised in R. Rothwell and W. Zegweld, *Technical Change and Employment*, London, 1979). Since it is unlikely, he writes, that the demand for small batch engineering products will double, never mind treble, by then, worldwide employment will drop to 50% of today's levels. Job loss will not be confined to shopfloor workers; designers and draughtspersons will also be displaced. In compensation, however, Remmerswaal considers that the work of the remaining employees will be reorganised so that it will become more interesting, less monotonous, less dangerous and more integrated.

There are good reasons to be sceptical of Remmerswaal's predictions (and his are not unusual in their claims of drastic employment reduction within 15 years). For example, various studies of the labour-displacing effects of NC machines—pointed to in the 1960s as likely to lead to a dramatic reduction in employment—have suggested that employment levels do not fall as fast as expected, if at all. Overall, the proportion of craft workers in the total workforce has·not altered very much. But, of course, one cannot take the effects of the slow spread of NC machines over the last twenty years as evidence for future effects, particularly in a period of restructuring. Some sectors of the engineering industry *have* seen a decline in the number and proportion of skilled machine setters and operators. From 1965 to 1975 skilled craftsworkers and supervisors in machine tool manufacture declined from 40,000 to 28,000. Though this drop can be attributed to the decline of the British machine tool industry, the changing proportion of craftworkers in the workforce—from 49.5% to 42.1%—cannot be explained in this way.

The potential for cheap computers and electronic machine control systems to raise the productivity and cheapen the products of small batch production engineering is a long-term one that will only be realised after a prolonged period of worldwide industrial restructuring. Machines and machine components have to be produced in small batches because, compared to individual consumer products, not many of them are needed. The production of a wide range of machines in one factory is inherently complex.

To sum up: there are strong economic reasons to force a rationalisation of small batch engineering, should the appropriate computer technologies be developed. However, in the next 10 to 15 years only the largest shops producing the smallest range of products will feel the pressure to introduce fully automated technology that requires no workers. This pressure will threaten jobs and skills of all types of small batch production workers—draughtspersons, craftworkers and machine operators. In principle, fully fledged computer-aided production could drastically reduce employment in all small batch engineering turning it into a process-like industry. This is still, however, just a dream of production engineers and computer manufacturers. Developments in microelectronics bring the fulfillment of that dream closer but do not necessarily make it imminent.

# 7
# Robots

*Hand built by robot* — Advertisement for a Fiat car.
*Your obedient servant . . . a robot to paint your products perfectly all day. All year. All right.* — Advertisement for a robot.

## What are robots?

Most people's conception of a robot comes from the science fiction vision of an exact substitute for a human being. This idea has tended to cloud assessments of real robots. There has been either a fatalistic tendency to believe that those robots in use today are much more advanced than is the case, or to think that robots are a complete fiction. Both of these views are dangerous for those who wish to control the use and development of robots.

A normal machine is confined to executing the single task for which it has been designed, and this is true no matter how automatic the machine is. A robot is distinguished by its flexibility; it is a general purpose, or universal machine, whose dexterity and versatility enables it to perform many different types of task. For example, a robot now in use in foundries can take hold of a hot casting, turn and then plunge it into a cooling bath. After that it can turn again and hold the casting up to a sensitive screen to do a preliminary quality-control check, before putting it onto a conveyor belt. The same robot is sufficiently flexible that, with suitable changes to its peripheral equipment, it can be used to unload a plastic injection moulding machine, or to spot weld the metal panels of a car. A robot which has mechanical joints and an arm, imitates human mechanical performance more closely than other machines.

Current robots have four elements: *a power unit* which is either hydraulic, pneumatic or electrical; *a control unit; a mechanical structure* with joints which can move in several directions and which is powered under the instructions of the control unit, to operate *a tool*, the working part, which may be, for example, a gripper with a wrist, a tube for spraying, or a spot welding gun.

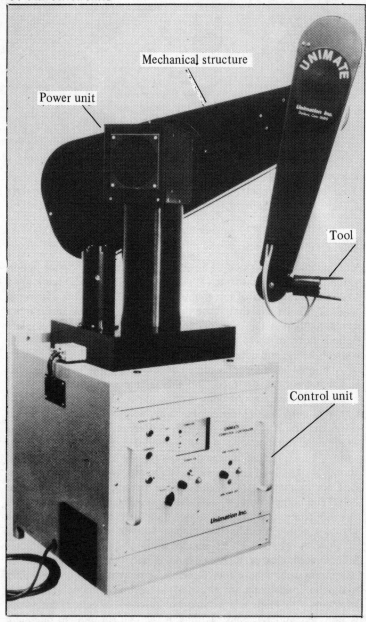

Unimation's pioneering Unimate: five years and $12 million in development for the first general purpose robot.

## The development of the robot

Modern industrial robots have been used commercially since 1962. Robots emerged from several areas of research. *Numerically controlled machine tools* were one move towards general purpose machines since small batches of machined parts could be produced more flexibly (see Chapter 6 on small batch production). *Remote manipulation machines* were developed in the late 1940s and early 1950s for the nuclear and space programmes. Advances in *control technology*, such as improved information processing, made it possible to design remote manipulation machines which could operate autonomously. Finally, *pick and place machines*, which could load and unload work stations, can also be seen as ancestors of robots.

All of these, together with the expertise developed during and after the second world war in servo theory (the theory of remotely assisting mechanical movement through feedback), in mechanical engineering and in hydraulics, formed the basis for the growth of a robot industry.

More recently, the most important development has been the introduction of microprocessors and minicomputers into control units. Such control units have allowed more complex tasks to be performed, and have made the units cheaper. It is estimated that the control unit has dropped from about 80% to about 20% of the cost of a robot in the last five to ten years. Robot systems have been able to maintain their real price over the last ten years as wage rates have increased.

Robots, like numerically controlled machine tools, come between hand tools which are used for the smallest batches, and inflexible, purpose built machines which are employed for large volume production. As wage rates rise and robots become mass produced, the use of robots will grow. There is now an economic justification for them in more and more applications.

## The growth of the robot industry

The first company to make and sell robots was Unimation Incorporated, in 1962. Its robot, and that of the other US pioneer, AMF, was designed for general loading and unloading applications in factories. Unimation was a small company set up around a robot inventor, Devol, who had worked as an aerospace engineer. Unimation received $12 million of venture capital over five years to develop it from two medium sized companies, one of which, Condec

Corporation, now owns the company. American Machine Foundry (AMF), a big US company, diversified into robot production from leisure activities, from their interests in remote manipulation systems like bowling.

The early years were much bleaker than expected. The only application that kept Unimation going was unloading hot castings from dies. Then in 1970 Unimation installed its first spot welding robot, the Unimate, in a General Motors car factory. It was this application which brought Unimation its first profits in 1975.

The expanding market for spot welding robots in the automobile industry has brought other companies into the robot industry, including car companies. Renault, Volkswagen, Kuka (West German), Comau (an Italian company linked to Fiat), and Mitsubishi all now produce robots themselves.

A medium-sized Norwegian company called Trallfa produced the first paint spraying robot in 1969. Trallfa manufactured garden wheelbarrows and painting them was considered a particularly dirty job. The company was hit by labour shortages and health and safety regulations. It researched possible ways of mechanising and eventually produced its own robot. Its robots are now considered the best for paint and enamel spraying. Trallfa's marketing success in this area has brought competitors into the spraying robot market. Examples are Nordson, a US automatic paint machinery specialist, Hall in the UK and Hitachi in Japan.

Because of these successes, the first optimistic efforts of Unimation and AMF to produce a totally flexible robot to fit every application has changed to making robots designed for a smaller range of applications. Flexibility is retained within a more restricted range. Thus the increasing market for arc-welding robots since 1976 has given Trallfa, Asea (a large Swedish company), BOC and Hall Automation (UK), Unimation and Kawasaki (a large Japanese industrial organisation), the opportunity to design robots for arc welding.

More recently, some large machine tool companies like Cincinnati-Milacron (US) and Fujitsu-Fanuc (Japan) have sunk large amounts of capital into R & D efforts to develop robots to load and unload machines.

Robots are still built in small batches of from one to twenty, using artisanal production techniques. The biggest company, Unimation, only manufactures 40 machines a month. Many companies are making no profit or only a very small amount. Some are spending significantly on R & D, the more advanced with state support in most countries.

Until last year, all commercial robots were described as first generation robots since they had no sensors to see or feel. The largest recent effort in R & D work has been to produce a robot with simple sensing. Simple sensors can, for example, check whether a part is correctly oriented. Others can increase the accuracy of attempts to put objects into holes with fine tolerance. Such robots are essential for automatic assembly work.

Olivetti jumped the gun in 1973 when it first launched the Sigma robot, but this pioneering attempt has not sold well. Finally, last year, Unimation put the Programmable Universal Machine for Assembly, Puma, robot on the market. Developed with General Motors, it is described as a 1½-generation robot, since it has simple sensing and can be directly programmed to do simple tasks like putting windscreen washers together, partially assemble armatures and screw light bulbs into car dashboards. Unimation is making fifteen a month, has orders for 200 and will soon start production in Britain.

Most of the state support for robotics in the US, Japan and Germany is in the area of sensing and automatic assembly. Texas Instruments and IBM in the US, and Fujitsu-Fanuc, Kawasaki and Hitachi in Japan are all rumoured to have sensing assembly robots that are either near to commercial viability or already in internal company use.

From rather small-scale entrepreneurial activities the robot industry has become organised in technologically rich subsidiaries of large companies who are increasingly prepared to sink capital into what is seen as a potential mushrooming market in the 1980s. Most informed forecasts suggest that in the late 1980s well-tried simple assembly robots will be in use for a wide range of assembly tasks in factories.

## Workers' low resistance to early robot applications

World robot use was estimated at only 8,000 in 1978. Japan used 3,000, the USA 2,500 and Western Europe 2,000. Within Western Europe, Sweden and West Germany used 600 each, Italy 400 and Britain only 70. World use is increasing rapidly. Perhaps 3,000 robots were produced in 1979, which means that the number is increasing at 35% a year. Important applications so far have been those of spot and arc welding; paint and enamel spraying; and the simple machine unloading of metal castings, presses, and of plastics from injection moulding machines. Only a few assembly operations have been automated.

When this first generation of paint spraying, welding and foundry-work robots has been installed, health and safety reasons have often been given as the principal explanation by factory management. Of course, dirty jobs are often defined as such by managements only when automation is possible. Management thus has most control over what is defined as a dirty job to be replaced. The majority of robots in Britain have been installed because managements could not keep workers in particularly dirty jobs for the wages they were willing to pay. One said 'our labour problems were very much increased in spraying. People didn't like the working conditions and this was reflected in difficulties of recruitment, absenteeism and a high rate of labour turnover of 30% a year'. But in Fiat the cleanest parts of the factory are where the robots are. The parts in which people work are dirtier.

The introduction of robots has usually increased productivity and improved the quality of products. Managements have sometimes been surprised at the large productivity increases that can be achieved (200-600%) and at the increased supervision and control they have over production. It is not for nothing that advertisements describe robots with such phrases as 'In this family everyone works for a living' and 'Versatile, tireless, accurate, dependable, the new, all-round factory helpmate'. In one company the number of workers in the enamel spraying section was decreased from 16 to 2. In yet another electrical appliance factory management installed robots in one section with a pliable trade union shop steward, but not in another with stronger stewards. The section with robots finished up with only one-half of the labour of that without robots. In all of these companies, there were no sackings, but transfers and natural wastage.

Several companies cited as an advantage that robotised jobs required fewer skills of the human workers. The problem of recruiting skilled labour was eliminated as unskilled labour could be substituted. A disadvantage was that robot maintenance required electrical and electronic skills which their mechanical maintenance technicians lacked.

Robots have tended to be installed in ones and twos into factories in Britain, and they have met only very low resistance from workers. This has made it very difficult for workers' organisation to control the new equipment. The same was true of the introduction of numerically controlled machine tools in the 1960s. Phil Higgs, a member of the Amalgamated Union of Engineering Workers at Rolls Royce, has said that 'with the introduction of nc machine tools in 1968 the local convenors and stewards sought help from their

national officers. However we still [1979] haven't received a reply
. . . our problems were made even more difficult, in fact, because the
machines were introduced piecemeal'. He also described the
demarcation dispute which arose with members of the Technical and
Supervisory Staffs, 'TASS, or rather certain members of TASS went
behind the back of the shop floor and made an agreement with
management that handed over the exclusive programming rights for
the nc machines. The result was that the three nc machines were
introduced, at enormous expense, but were then blacked for six
months by the AUEW . . .' As a result of this dispute machine tool
operators were taught nc programming at Rolls Royce and the
manual and staff unions have worked more closely together.

One large Japanese company recently introduced robots after
carrying out a campaign to persuade workers that the robots were
their tools. Workers received a short course in programming the
robots. On their introduction the robots were programmed by the
line workers. There is little evidence of this happening in Britain.

## *Robot lines and workers*

Although management has often given labour resistance as a reason
for the lack of robot use in Britain this is difficult to substantiate.
Joe Engelberger, the head of Unimation and spokesperson for the
unofficial robot lobby, said in 1979 that Britain was far behind in
robotics. Trade union resistance could not be blamed for Britain's
lack of robot use; nor could lack of expertise. Tom Brock,
Executive Secretary of the British Robot Association, has said that
union leaders are better informed than management.

Worker resistance has so far been low. But the installation of
robots in larger numbers may change that. Spot-welding robot lines
indicate what will be possible in some automated assembly tasks in
the late 1980s. The new BL Mini Metro is to be assembled on a
robotised line that is due to begin operations in August 1980 at
Longbridge. Negotiations with the unions took place during the
operation of a partnership scheme between unions and management
set up in 1976. This was one of the industrial democracy schemes of
the 1974 Labour government. The Longbridge Joint Shop Stewards
Committee was given full information about the proposed automation and it participated in a decision to go for a semi-automated
system with 28 Unimate welding robots. The plan at that time
envisaged no job loss because car production would be increased. A
system of team working linked to a mixture of automated and conventional technology was adopted by unions and management after

Programmable robots, like BOC's welder, will permanently take skill from workers and embed it in the machine.

two years of detailed discussions. The arrival of Michael Edwardes coincided with negotiations about implementing the agreed changes.

The main demand by workers was for higher wages. 'The Works Committee had no intention that Longbridge, which would become the most efficient car factory in Britain, would remain the lowest paid.' Management refused these demands. Shop stewards believed as early as April 1979, well before Robinson's sacking, that management refusal of these demands signalled a change 'from participation to management by command following the appointment of Michael Edwardes'.

Demarcation disputes arose over the introduction of the new technology at BL. Some craft workers divided themselves from the other workers and the unions. 'We've got craftsmen being trained on the Unimate machines and refusing to be involved with us on negotiating how we· are going to man it because they are being bloody minded . . . we keep raising the question with them. Now we see the need to negotiate in detail what we are going to do with this new technology so that we can build in that essence of control which is absolutely essential and we are going to be successful only to the degree that we can unite all the groups of workers who are going to be involved. If we are unable to build that unity then management will play off groups against groups: they've done it already between the electricians and the toolroom where they were arguing about the teach-control . . . a production operator can be trained to set the programme on these Unimate welding machines . . . it doesn't need a skilled maintenance fitter to set the limits.' (Derek Robinson and Jack Adams interviewed in *Comment*, Vol. 16 (1979), pp. 250-54).

This sort of information on work practices around new technology puts a different light on the BL struggle. It is a fact that the Fiat robot automation was of part of a line with exceptionally strong worker power. The introduction of the Fiat Robogate system at Rivolta did not appear to have a clear financial rationale in the short term. It cost £13 million, an estimated £3 million more than a conventional system, and required twice as much factory space. The workforce was cut by 100, from 125 to 25 but this only saved about £500,000 in labour costs. This means a pay-back period of more than six years–which is much higher than the three years that is usually considered the maximum for robot installations.

## The British state and robot development

The dispute at BL is probably the first in Britain that is even indirectly linked with robot technology. There will be more, given the recent state initiatives in robot technology and the increase in robot use. British use of robots was low until 1979 and it even seems to have declined between 1975 and 1978 at a time when the number in use in most other advanced capitalist countries was increasing.

Recent reports have pinpointed the necessity for Britain to increase its resources in robotics. One report states: 'It is vital that the UK should proceed rapidly with the introduction of these devices. Failure to apply them will result in our industries being progressively less able to compete with either the high productivity industrialised countries or with the low labour cost countries . . . to meet the immediate need it will be necessary to rely on imported robots, but there are good opportunities to build a British robot industry, making use of our skills in engineering design, remote handling and software.'

Governments in other countries have already moved to support research in robot development. In West Germany, for example, the government alone spent £50 million on support between 1974 and

1977. The United States ICAM programme involves funding of $130 million to promote industrial robots in small batch production.

There is now evidence of the beginnings of a coherent strategy. A Science Research Council (SRC) committee chaired by Derek Roberts (recently appointed head of GEC Research) has picked out robotics as one of four areas linked with computing that should have special attention. 'The panel considers that there is an urgent need for a co-ordinated programme of research and development in the field of industrial robotics. Current activity in the UK (both industrial and academic) is disturbingly weak when compared with the situation in USA, Germany and Japan.'

State aid for robotics increased in 1979 from almost nothing to an announced £2.5 million over one and a half to three years. Over £1 million of this will come from the SRC for research and development, mostly involving joint programmes between universities and industry. The SRC already has a full-time co-ordinator for this programme. He has been seconded from research at Oxford University on image analysis to the SRC's own Rutherford Laboratory. He has proposed a SRC programme integrating research in the areas of remote handling, computing, robot sensing (visual and tactile) and software, and hopes to get £750,000 a year for it from 1980. This could play a key role in integrating different fields of research that have previously been isolated.

The Department of Industry (DOI) has already provided £1.5 million for robotics. The Production Engineering Research Association (PERA) received £450,000 from the DOI and the National Research Development Corporation (NRDC). It has gone to PERA's new Director-General Professor Heginbotham, who until this recent appointment, used to head Britain's biggest university research group in robot technology at Nottingham's Production Engineering Department. PERA will carry out feasibility studies into robot applications which will be subsidised by 50% for all customers. The National Engineering Laboratory (NEL) has been given £330,000 for research into possible applications for robots, including welding. The Welding Institute has £170,000 for research into robotic welding.

Finally the DOI encouraged Unimation to assemble its advanced Puma robot in Britain. Of the £1.5 million required to set up assembly in Britain, £660,000 will be provided by the state: £220,000 as a grant by the DOI and £440,000 as a loan by the NRDC. The NRDC loan is unusually large and it required statutory approval by the DOI. The assembly of Puma robots in Britain will be the first time that they have been manufactured outside the USA. Unimation for its part was keen to manufacture in the UK because it has been given firm indications of large orders by two large UK companies. The Secretary of State for Industry, Keith Joseph, therefore seems in practice to have accepted the need for a robotics programme even though he has publicly claimed otherwise.

The link between government and industry has been further strengthened with the GEC-Marconi takeover of Hall Automation, until this year Britain's only robot manufacturer. The head of GEC's corporate research laboratory, Derek Roberts, was chairman of the SRC report referred to earlier. GEC's Technical Director, Sir Robert Clayton, who recently became a board member of the National Enterprise Board announced the takeover of Hall in December 1979. He explained that with the takeover GEC would jump two years in the race for an automatic assembly robot. Two months later, the cabinet's scientific advisory council, ACARD, published the report of a working party chaired by Clayton that advocated further state support for computer aided design and manufacture.

## *Robots are not science fiction*

Robots are not science fiction. They are already in factories but they are nothing like the invincible science fiction robots. They are dumb and cannot see or talk. 'Hand built by robot'? No. Welded and painted by robot but still assembled by humans. Many products will be redesigned by the late 1980s so that they can be assembled by robots, but for some complex products this will be difficult. The adverts reinforce the fiction that robots are invincible and cannot be resisted or controlled and that is dangerous.

## *Postscript: robotics at Fords*

In June 1980, after a close management study of Japanese techniques in motor manufacturing, Ford Motors (UK) announced a shift of policy: extensive manning cuts, together with a higher degree of automation and robotisation – all to be achieved by bypassing trade union channels of consultation and consensus. At the time of writing, the trade union response is still being formulated.

# 8
# Process

*Whose progress?*

Are workers' skills and wages up-graded in an industry as increasingly advanced technology is applied to production? The experience of workers who have actually been affected by new technology strongly suggests the opposite. However, the myth of technological up-grading has been with us for many years and is now being used by civil servants, politicians and media experts as part of an ideological offensive to sell microelectronics to the working class. According to the government think-tank, new technology, despite some transitional problems, is good news, because the industrial worker 'will have the opportunity to acquire new skills and the freedom associated with white-collar work' (Central Policy Review Staff, *Social and Employment Implications of Microelectronics*, HMSO, 1978).

The process industries are important because in the 1950s and 1960s oil refineries and chemical plants were the first examples of very capital-intensive production that was highly automated or, more accurately, mechanised. It has often been said that the up-grading effect of advanced production technology on the skills and status of workers is demonstrated in these industries:

> The case of the continuous process industries, particularly the chemical industry, shows that automation increases the worker's control over his work process and checks the further division of labour and the growth of large factories. The result is meaningful work in a more cohesive, integrated industrial climate . . . as employees in automated industries gain a new dignity from responsibility and a sense of individual function (Robert Blauner, *Alienation and Freedom*, University of Chicago, 1964).

Microelectronics will enable more industries to achieve continuous-flow production which is what characterises process industries. It is therefore important to examine the experience of technology and work in existing process industries to see if such an up-grading has really occurred and what difference microelectronics is likely to make.

## *The process industries*

The process industries do not assemble objects, they process materials. In so far as a material such as a gas, a powder or a liquid or molten metal can be treated as a fluid, a continuous flow can be set up. The material is piped through various stages and by mixing and using pressure and chemical reaction it is transformed into a product such as plastic, steel, cement, glass, chemicals or artificial fibres.

This fluidification of the process allows the plant to be linked as one huge machine. Material enters at one end and the product flows into tanks or drums at the other, so that the workforce may not touch or even see its product. A plant will have three kinds of workers: operators, maintenance workers and ancillary workers who feed in the raw materials and take away the product.

## *A 'new working class'?*

Pipe-fitters, truck drivers and mechanics are not particular to the process industries but process control is. It is the process operators who are said to have been up-graded and some sociologists have pointed to them as being examples of a 'new working class'.

Operators work as teams, in shifts, to control the multi-million pound plant. Its operation has to be co-ordinated by balancing temperatures, pressures and flows so as to maximise the throughput while maintaining quality and ensuring that it operates safely. There are start-ups, shutdowns, batch changes from one product to another and blockages and occasional emergencies to be dealt with. Process operators have to be alert, knowledgeable and intelligent. They must know and be able to anticipate the behaviour of the particular plant intimately. Often it can be important to understand the significance of noises, of changes in the colour and texture of the product and the movement of dials and indicators.

Operators do not serve apprenticeships or hold certificates but are classed as unskilled workers. Pay is above average for manual work but this is accounted for by the unsocial hours, the overtime and the unpleasant environment, that is, the conditions of work, not the level or responsibility, initiative and knowledge that are said to justify the status and rewards of white-collar workers. Process technology may have created the skill of process control, but the employers have not rewarded it.

Managements, however, do recognise the power operators have to control and disrupt production. First, this control can be a stoppage by operators, which will shut down the plant immediately. Strikes are less common than in, for example, shipbuilding or motors, but they are financially damaging and very effective, so the strike threat is a powerful reserve weapon.

Second, process control is a group task, since the plant is linked as one big machine. It has therefore not been possible for management to use the classic techniques of scientific management, that is to achieve a minute sub-division of jobs all controlled through detailed management instructions, so that the work is fragmented and the workers are isolated from each other. The need for understanding and initiative by the operators means that management has to try to motivate workers and obtain their co-operation by persuasion and leave the shift team considerable autonomy.

The spread of the shop-steward system has allowed power to be shared through negotiation in return for reliable and continuous production. The growth of operators' collective power on the plant could be tolerated by employers during the 1960s and early 1970s, because profits were sufficiently high to enable them to rule by concession and to put up with lower levels of productivity than were being achieved in other countries. Under these conditions, process operators were able to make gains on pay, holidays, sickness, grading and safety and to establish considerable autonomy in controlling the work process.

## Crisis in the process industries

The era of high profits in process industries ended in 1973 with the onset of the recession. The sudden fall in demand for chemicals, steel, glass and plastics resulted in a huge world-wide amount of unused capacity. The price of most raw materials, especially oil, jumped.

The crisis is illustrated by the artificial fibre industry. Fibres use oil as raw material. Production has been contracting and moving out of the UK. Production in the US is favoured by the lower cost of oil. The largest British producer, ICI, showed a loss for its fibre division of £13 million in 1978 and £33 million in 1979. This led to large-scale redundancies.

These technologically advanced industries only provided more secure jobs during the era of general economic expansion. With the onset of recession, the very high ratio of capital equipment to labour (as high as £1 million of plant per employee) makes it easy for workers to produce themselves out of a job.

*Table 8.1*: ICI Fibres Division — a shrinking workforce

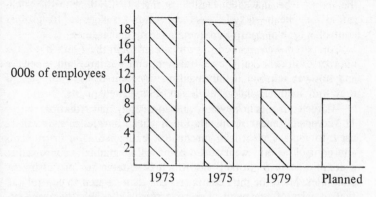

Industrial relations in the process industries changed dramatically, as millions of pounds worth of plant was junked and thousands of jobs were destroyed. In 1980 the steel industry had its first ever national strike. The national officer for the chemical industry in the General and Municipal Workers' Union, the largest for process workers, warned delegates to the 1977 national conference:

There are those who seek to exploit our record by means of a 'hatchet job' on manning levels and who seek our compliance with indiscriminate redundancy plans . . .The social consequences of investment policies, coupled with the export of capital could quickly transform industrial relations in the chemical industry into a quagmire of disputes and confrontation.

### Who controls control?

Capitalism's answer to low profitability in the process industries is to close plants that make a loss and launch a cost-cutting drive against the remainder. Wages are not a large part of total costs in such a capital-intensive kind of production but the squeeze on profits makes cuts in the wage bill very desirable. To get the same output with fewer people implies further automation of control.

Another and more powerful link between low profitability and automation comes from the drive to raise the efficiency of plant performance. Firms can no longer afford to get increased output and efficiency by building ever-larger new plant. They need to get more output, more consistent quality and better use of energy and raw materials by tighter control of existing plant. This tighter control cannot, however, be gained by management while human operators control a plant.

Reducing the number of operators and the autonomy of those that remain became more feasible in the late 1970s with the application of cheap flexible microprocessor intelligence to process control, a type of control programmable by management.

Computers were applied to process control in the 1960s but had a number of drawbacks. The central computer was large and expensive and not yet reliable. It only paid management to use computers if they were incorporated in the design of large, new plants.

Microelectronics however, create an entirely new situation.

1. Microelectronic instrumentation is cheap and reliable. It will be used to replace electrical, mechanical and pneumatic instruments and controls as they wear out. A plant will be gradually converted to a common electronic language which is suitable for processing by computer. Micro or mini computers can then be used to control particular parts of the plant. The next stage is to link these and co-ordinate their performance with a larger computer. After this, perhaps, links could be established with other plants or with company design and record computers. With satellite communications the network could even reach an overseas head office!

2. Each stage is fairly cheap; it can be experimented with and a payback realised before moving on to the next level of computerisation.

3. The hardware is in units, which can be linked up in many ways and the shape of the whole system is determined by the software. Automatic control can be fitted to an existing plant and does not have to wait for old plant to become obsolete, nor does it depend on an upturn in the market to justify investment on new plants.

4. The software can be developed as the engineers learn more about the behaviour of the plant and strategies for optimising performance. If it records how operators deal with unusual situations the computer can permanently extend the area where human intervention is unnecessary.

Suppliers are working to simplify programming by producing software in packages that plant managers and engineers can use to program their own plant without having to pay for expensive expertise. Access to the program can be controlled according to a person's position in a company's hierarchy. With the appropriate key or password, managers or engineers can make major program changes, supervisors lesser changes and operators can be restricted to routine inputs following a programmed path. In an emergency, a more senior employee can cut in on the operator from the main terminal.

*Table 8.2*: Predicted market for process control instrumentation in Western Europe.

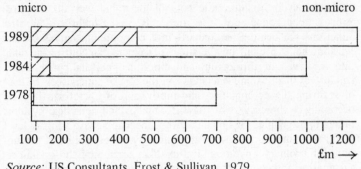

*Source*: US Consultants, Frost & Sullivan, 1979.

The timing of operations is important. On batch plants, a shift will often prolong the production of a batch, so that they will not have to start another before going home. Computerised control provides management with a record of everything that has happened in a plant including the pace at which operators work, an area previously under their own control.

### Whose intelligence?

The increasingly complex task of plant control could be tackled by acknowledging the existing skills of operators and training them in the new skills necessary to use a computer, but as a tool under their control. Employers, however, are working to close off this option. They want to increase the self-acting character of control systems, to exclude operator interference as much as possible and so save on the costs of training operators while reserving control over a plant for managers, engineers and supervisors.

A contradiction exists between excluding operators from the routine running of a plant and yet having to rely on them to deal with unusual events that go beyond the capability of the computer. A recent example was the failure of the automatic system at the Three Mile Island nuclear power station in 1979. The US Nuclear Regulatory Commission report on the accident said that 'Confronted with 200 alarms and an over-abundance of situations they had not been trained to deal with, operators at the Three Mile Island contributed inadvertently to making the situation worse by their actions'. Having come so far in eliminating workers, the difficulty of re-establishing effective operator intervention in an emergency can then be used to justify total automation, or at least to make computer operation a function reserved for staff engineers.

These levels of automatic control are some way off for most process operations but the trend is well-established: control functions are being separated off into computer programs so that without being present on the site management can control the plant and the levels of throughput and monitor operators' performance. One effect of this trend is a change in the role of supervisors. Instead of securing the co-operation and motivation of operators, they are becoming technicians who have to understand technical systems rather than people. This means fewer supervisors, with a higher level of formal education and a correspondingly lower chance of promotion for ordinary operators. Rather than upgrading the operators, automation and computerisation are likely to increase polarisation as operators are deskilled and the new conceptual skills are concentrated in the hands of managerial, technical and supervisory staff.

However, these trends are likely to be opposed and the final form of the automated process plant will in part be shaped by the workers.

1. Process operators are well organised and have the power to disrupt production; they may refuse to operate new technology if it seems to undermine their position significantly.

2. Rising unemployment, and the knowledge that they can be easily replaced from the dole queue but may not find another job, is making operators more active in defending their position in production.

3. With microelectronic technology there will be many possible ways of distributing information, control, co-ordination and initiative between operators, managers and machines. Workers can argue about that as they have done in the past.

One choice that exists is distributed control in which operators use terminals scattered around the plant. Will this kind of system be used to isolate workers from each other, so that they can only communicate through paths that have been determined by management? Or can it become a system for operators to talk both to the computer and also to each other, so retaining group interaction and control of the plant? The answers to this kind of question will depend on the bargaining strength of the operators.

*'Someone will have to look after it though'*

The number of process operators in a plant is roughly equalled by maintenance workers such as electricians, pipe-fitters and instrument mechanics. In the past, substituting equipment for human skill has increased the number of maintenance personnel but this will no longer be true. Microelectronics is intended to cut the number of maintenance workers and to reduce their power.

A major headache for management in the process industries has been the shortage of instrument mechanics. So many instruments have remained unserviced and out of action, that there has sometimes had to be a reversion to control techniques directly based on human labour. In 1978 this problem led to the complete shutdown of ICI plants on Teeside.

Companies that trained instrument mechanics have found them poached by other companies. High wages in the North-Sea oil and other related industries have made the shortage worse for others. Government pay policy has kept the wages of skilled workers down, especially in the public sector, and workers have taken jobs that did not employ their particular skills.

There is a shortage of all types of maintenance staff, not only instrument mechanics, and this means that management cannot increase the intensity of work through tighter supervision, nor can it challenge the demarcation between trades, for fear of people leaving. With the collapse of profitability, the lack of managerial control over maintenance departments is no longer tolerable for firms faced by a desperate need to cut costs.

Management's answer is not to train more workers with the appropriate skills but to use microelectronic technology to deskill maintenance work. Electrical, mechanical and pneumatic instruments have many intricate parts. Microelectronic-based instruments have far fewer parts, none of which involve physical movement. They are designed in modular form, so that faulty sections can be easily replaced from stock. Faults can be identified by the system itself. Faulty parts may be cheap enough to throw away or they may be sent back to the supplier for repair. These developments will make the mechanical skills of instrument mechanics obsolete.

A more general line of attack against the craft character of maintenance work is to systemise it through terotechnology, which is the use of work-study techniques to develop strategies for cheapening, deskilling and speeding up maintenance work in every industry. In ICI Organic Chemicals Division, each plant is collecting information about the performance of maintenance workers, and this is stored in a computer and processed to find ways of saving time on various jobs. The results are to be fed into the design process so that new plant will have much lower maintenance requirements than that which it replaces.

Another way of reducing the power of a maintenance department is to use productivity deals to break down the distinction between maintenance and other work. For example, if process operators have less to do because of automated control, they could also do routine maintenance jobs that have been deskilled through the introduction of modular instrumentation and the application of terotechnology. There is a trend towards merging operators and maintenance workers into a homogenous, deskilled work force that is cheap and easily trained and which could be replaced from the dole queue with little difficulty. Technical skills could be reserved for a small number of elite technicians and supervisors who would be separated by pay and status from other workers. Non-routine repair and maintenance work could be done by outside contractors.

## Donkey work

At least a third of the people working at most process plants will be ancillary workers who feed in the raw material and remove the finished product. If the product is liquid, these may be mainly tanker drivers but a solid product can result in labour-intensive, bagging and loading work. As a result of the work and conditions it is hard to get people to do this. There is a high turnover and workers are often off sick. If they stop work, the whole plant may have to face shutdown.

Management's long-term solution appears to be a jump from muscle-power straight to robots. If a robot can be made robust enough, it can replace a person who is being used as a robot. From management's point of view, this would eliminate the unreliable human factor from this end of production and link up with the automated plants. Robots are already being used experimentally for this type of work. To abolish heavy, tedious labour, working in a dusty, hazardous environment is desirable, but the technology will be used to throw out workers whose health is already damaged onto the dole queue.

## Who is to benefit?

Process plants in the 1950s and '60s, although very capital-intensive, were based on high-level mechanisation, rather than automation. The skills that were necessary gave maintenance workers and process operators a level of control that is now seen as an obstacle by management. It wishes to take the next step towards full automation that has been made possible by microelectronics. Process industries, therefore, do not demonstrate that the introduction of advanced technology into production upgrades workers. On the contrary, the current stage of automation suggests that opportunities to deskill workers will definitely be used by employers.

Computers could perform routine functions such as sampling the product, maintaining temperatures and pressures and identifying faults and blockages, and be matched with workers' initiative, imagination and problem-solving ability. The reduction in routine work could enable working hours to be reduced and pay to be increased through higher output. However, managers running the process industries are unlikely to concede this. Cheap, machine intelligence is likely to be used to deskill and substitute for human ability as a means of increasing the direct control of management over the work process.

This analysis is not meant to imply that workers will passively accept automation. Process workers are likely to resist and may find ways of dealing with microelectronic technology that other groups of workers can use.

The strategy that most process workers are likely to face will be:

1. Designing plants that are highly automated and which require only minimum maintenance.

2. Introducing automatic controls in a piecemeal fashion into existing plants; no redundancy agreements will be made but at the time of the next financial crisis the plant will be said to be over-staffed and closure will be threatened unless redundancies are made.

3. Allowing other plants to deteriorate *without* new equipment, so that low productivity can be used as an excuse for closure. The lost output will be available from the increased capacity of the auto-mated plants.

One response has been the demand of the GMWU for an end to systematic overtime and progress towards a 35-hour week, with com-pensatory pay rises. Another is the opposition to contract labour, in order to keep work within the company, as occurred with the Shell tanker drivers' dispute in 1979.

The problem, however, is not just numbers of jobs, for a job that remains but loses content is, in the long-run, less secure. So it will be necessary to get involved in bargaining over the *form* of the new technology. One answer could be to oppose any new system until its implications have been understood and alternatives have been argued over.

# 9
# Motors

In 1978, the 'Year of the Microprocessor', the question of new technology, microelectronic or otherwise, was wholly missing from the Transport and General Workers' Union 17-page wage claim for the manual workers of the Ford Motor Company. The four-page discussion of shorter working-time that it contained was wholly divorced from any consideration at all of the impact of new technologies. It was as if the Ford manual unions did not consider new technology as an issue for collective bargaining at this stage. From this we could conclude that new technology was not a burning issue for the *direct production* workforce at Ford – and therefore for the rest of the UK motor industry working class, since Ford tends to be the pacesetter. Such a conclusion is supported by conversations with Ford manual workers, who feel that they do not face an on-slaught of new technologies. Ford in the UK is not about to 'do a FIAT' – in fact, in recent company film-shows on the subject, Ford has been specific that it does *not* intend to go as far as Fiat in line-automation and robotisation. (The situation was very different on the white-collar side at Fords, as the 1978 Technical, Administrative and Supervisory Section Agreement on New Technology showed; that, however, is outside the scope of this chapter.)

In February 1980, an American union advisor on the subject of new technology came to Coventry, to advise the British car industry unions on the drastic impact of the new automation in the US auto sector. To summarise his argument:

* Robots which can fully inspect new car bodies in five minutes are now working in Ford's Lincoln motor plant, Detroit. The same job takes human workers up to four hours. Some motor industry managers are now predicting a halving of the US auto-sector work-force within the next 10 years. In 1979 the Ford unions were the first to bring the question of new machinery into collective bargaining. Three issues are at stake: job loss, job control and job power. Every part of the production process will soon be open to computer takeover. Total mechanisation of welding and paint-

spraying is expected within three years. Right at the start of the production process, draughtsmen's work has already been hit, for computers are being used to design dies—the steel forms used to stamp out the sheet-metal part of the car. And tape-fed numerical control machine tools automatically produce the panels. Almost 90% of GM's dies are now produced by computer. In unemployment terms, one-in-four US car workers is now out of work because of the slump in demand, the troubles of the giant Chrysler Corporation and the introduction of new machinery.

* Job control implications are serious. Using the new machines a foreman can monitor every minute of the worker's day and can pace the worker's work rate. At GM in Oklahoma City, workers clock in and out on a computer. Elsewhere, by watching a screen, a foreman can learn how fast workers are working and when they take breaks. GM's new robot system has been designed to replace workers in bench assembly. Humans will have a robot on either side of them, dictating work-speeds.

* Power also passes from the workers' hands, under the computer regime. Machinists at McDonnell Douglas Aerospace found that management could keep 60% of production going when they walked out. When GM die-makers struck, the firm simply took away the computer tapes and resumed production at another plant.

* In a massive *$100,000 million* investment programme, the US Big Three, Ford, GM and Chrysler, are planning to re-equip almost all of their car plants over the coming 5 years. What is happening in the USA prefigures what will happen in Britain. But Britain will not need to go through the same development processes. The most advanced forms will be introduced right away.

## Reasons for Britain's new technology time-lag

A complex system of factors must be explored to explain why new technologies are slow in coming in the direct-production side of the UK motor industry.

There is a time-lag before advanced technologies are transferred abroad in a finished form by imperialist countries. The technologies first need to be tried and tested in proximity to the research facilities and the skilled working class (technicians) that develop them.

Automation, and robotisation in particular, is at root related to the highest levels of workers' insubordination in direct production. The instances of workers' insubordination and control in the UK motor industry were well-advanced in the late 1960s and early 1970s

At assembly lines humans will have a robot on either side of them dictating work-speeds.

as part of an international cycle of auto workers' struggles that showed common themes, common forms of struggle and common forms of organisation. 1974 in particular, when labour market conditions were so favourable to the working class, was a high point at Ford-UK. However, UK in-plant struggles and contradictions have not reached the insurrectional extremities of the Italian Fiat workers, or the intensity of social breakdown of the US car factories in the aftermath of the Vietnam War and the risings of the black working class.

The type of labour upsurge represented by May '68 in France and the Hot Autumn of 1969 in Italy, was delayed for British car workers into the early 1970s. Its highest point seemed to coincide with the heady moments of the 1974 Elections that swept Labour back into office – the period of maximum confusion of the capitalist collective brain. Capital's response to this extension of workers' power was an *apparent* coming-to-terms with Social Democracy (in the form of Labour's reforming programme), masking the preparation of a *real* onslaught in terms of recession, plant closure, flight of capital and mass unemployment. On the one hand, uncertainties about the future of capitalism in Britain provided a disincentive to invest. On the other hand, capital would be prepared to invest only once the conditions for making a profit had been re-established. The re-establishment of those conditions has been the principal task of the period 1975-1980.

It would seem that lower levels of unionisation and in-plant control in the USA would make the introduction of new technologies relatively easier in America than in Britain. However, in Italy it has been precisely that strength of in-plant Union control of the labour process that has spurred automation; the new automation arises at least in part from a dialogue between labour and capital, about the necessity to humanise work and thereby raise social productivity. In Britain this debate is not at all advanced. At Ford, for instance, the Union response to the alienation of the lineworker is to demand more money, in the form of the Lineworker's Allowance (1978 TGWU Wage Claim) and more time off, rather than a radical revamping of the work environment.

British-based capital has, recently, been slow to adopt new technological advances. It rightly fears the ability of the working class to subvert new technologies and the payment and work systems that generally accompany them. For example, the introduction of Measured Day Work together with Power Loading in the coal mines, and the Containerisation in the docks, produced a dramatic drop in workers' productivity in the late 1960s and early 1970s.

## The Digitron system at Fiat-Mirafiori

For a specific example of assembly-line automation, we have taken the *Digitron* system at Fiat-Mirafiori. Fiat is now famous for its programme of automation for the 1980s. Fiat in Turin probably represents the highest point of the ongoing political confrontation between capital and labour in Europe. As such, the introduction of

Computerised control of the whole Fiat production process includes Robo-carriers (above), bolting, welding and final assembly.

this new machinery arises from, and gives rise to, a whole series of very profound considerations.

Fiat's policy of using highly automated plant for its car production began in the 1960s and is now the most advanced in the world. Fiat management has evolved important techological innovations, in its own words, 'to recover a fair margin or flexibility, which has been lost owing to worker disputes'. The following major initiatives have been taken by management.

1. Body welding shops have been equipped with robot spot welders.
2. Robots have been introduced for spray painting of the car at the Cassino Plant in Southern Italy.
3. Fully automatic electrocoating plant using powder has been installed at Termini Imerese replacing conventional painting.
4. Computerisation has occurred of the 'high lines' at Mirafiori.
5. Robogate carriers have been introduced in place of the conventional assembly line.

We shall describe in some detail the changes in the fourth of these.

The High Lines (also known as Cross Feed or Drop) is that section of the car assembly plant leading into the Final Lines, where the welded, painted body shell is brought in overhead and is dropped onto the engine and transmission unit, to be bolted together before going on to the Final Trim. It is a strong potential bottleneck in a car factory's production flow. It is a tricky area of co-ordination, requiring flexibility in the bringing-together of diverse models. It is an area where the exercise of workers' power can be effective and is a focal point of management's concern. (It is also an area where workers' sabotage is not unknown.)

The organisation of the labour process at this point can also be contentious, with options for management divide-and-rule. On one shift of the Dagenham Paint, Trim and Assembly Section in 1978, the topside workers were markedly white; the underside workers, working in pits underneath the car, were markedly Black and Asian. Underside-working involves the very unpleasant task of working with your arms raised above shoulder-height.

It is this section that the Fiat-Mirafiori management in Turin decided to automate with the Digitron system on the Fiat 131 line. Whereas other points of the cycle of production have been considerably automated in the past 10 years, this section of the line had seen few innovations as a result of the complexity of the operations involved. A Fiat company report explains the operations previously involved along this section of the line, and details the extreme fragmentation and complexity of jobs that need to be done:

> The body shells arrive on an overhead line. They are brought to the Assembly Lines from the Paint Shop. The Assembly Lines are divided into two distinct stretches: Trim and Assembly. The *Trim* (151 workers, excluding foremen) consists of four gangs: one gang fixes in the wiring loom; one fixes in windows; one fixes windscreens, petrol tanks etc. The *Assembly* consists of 98 workers, divided into six gangs, who fit (in sequence) the steering box, headlights, steering wheel etc. Each pair of workers carries out highly simplified, repetitive operations.
>
> Another gang is involved in unloading engines from the conveyor line. The engine is then fixed to the body shell, and the remaining assembly jobs are then completed (fixing electrical units, exhaust pipes etc.). The joining of the body shell and the engine involves bringing together two items that are brought on two separate lines, which are linked by a circular line known as the *towveyor*.

The organisation of the production process upstream and downstream of the Digitron has not been changed. But the important thing about Digitron is not the Robocarriers or the automatic bolting stations that comprise it, but the computerised control of this part of the production process which affects virtually the whole cycle of production. This control system is capable of guaranteeing, simultaneously, a greater flexibility of production; an improvement in the nature of the work (work pace, noise, possibility of teamwork); and tendency to increased vertical and horizontal control of production and of the workforce.

The Digitron system involves a complete, computerised transformation of this whole area of work, with the automatic preparation and joining together of Fiat 131 bodies and engine sub-assemblies. It consists of:

> * five fixed stations where the engine/transmission sub-assemblies are automatically bolted onto body shells;
>
> * a centralised depository, on five levels, where the engine and transmission sub-assemblies are brought from upstream production lines, and from where they can then be transported for fixing to body shells. These engine/transmission units are mounted on pallets;

* 32 automatic trucks – known as *Robocarriers* – which are electronically guided to their destination by a magnetic tracer buried under the floor surface. These Robocarriers operate between the upstream sections that provide the bodies and engines, linking them to the despatch points, the pallet depository, and the Final Assembly lines downstream;

* an automated, computerised information system that controls the operation of the plant stock control, movement of Robocarriers, input and output and job control;

* a reduction in the number of workers required, because screwing or bolting of the sub-assemblies, previously done by hand, is now done automatically.

Without going further into the operations of this new automated system, which is similar to the one in operation at Volvo-Kalmar, we can see some of the advantages for Fiat management. First, the assembly line can be eliminated at the meeting point of the two major production phases of the motor car, the engine and the body. Secondly, the resulting rationalisation into production 'modules' allows for greater flexibility of the production line. The ability to build up 'lungs', or stockpiles, reduces the sectional power of workers. This ability is provided by the flexibility of the computer-controlled Robocarriers, which are capable of rerouting in abnormal circumstances.

Thirdly, the introduction of fixed-station working within the overall continuous nature of the flow of production is a political intervention in the organisation of work, a step away from the assembly line towards group working. For example, the Robocarrier proceeds from one station to another under the command of the group of workers involved. Fourthly, there has been a partial recognition of Union demands regarding conditions of work. Noise levels have been reduced, and the lighting has improved with the elimination of overhead lines. Raised-arm bolting or screwing operations have been eliminated. Individual jobs have been re-designed, allowing a certain degree of independence to workers. And finally, job-loss, at least in the short term, has not been high in absolute terms, since the new system requires an expansion of the skilled and maintenance workforce.

## The politics of automation at Fiat

The recent restructuring at Fiat was like a period of post-war reconstruction. Some sections were functioning satisfactorily; others had to be virtually rebuilt from scratch, using new technologies, some of which were supplied by Fiat's own machine-tool subsidiary Comau. In this period Fiat *needed* the trade unions. They were delegated a function of mediating minor issues at plant level, and guaranteeing at least some productive activity while the restructuring was going ahead. At the same time workers were grateful to the unions for an apparent easing of workloads.

But this 'concordat' changed the nature of the union in the plant. For the union, the new automation was a step towards the 'new way of producing motor cars'—but it had its dangers. Shop stewards became more and more like foremen. They became involved in the problems of making the new systems work. Union officials developed a new language of 'technicalese' that separated them and their concerns from shop floor workers. And for what gains?

The only reason that Fiat introduced this automation was in order to break trade union control in the plants; to break the rigidity of the workforce; to remove the unions from their position of mediation between management and workers; to remove workers and unions from access to sources of information regarding production; and to transform the worker-producers into button-pushers, robbed of control. Management at Mirafiori said after they first used robots, 'This new way of working became "less hot" from the point of view of strikes compared to other body-welding shops'. Concretely, the changed relationship between workers and shop stewards has been so dramatic that many stewards have resigned, unable to cope with the contradictions.

These arguments have been fully spelled out by the revolutionary left in Italy. The unions and the Communist Party, on the other hand, say that those who oppose automation are Luddites. The unions say that they have fought for years in order to lessen the burden of workloads in the factory. The new technology represents an advance in this direction. Also, collective bargaining had reached a point where very few further advances could be made in the context of the traditional assembly line; the only further option was for a transformation of work; and in order to alter the organisation of production, automation is bound to be needed. The unions accept progress, on condition that they keep it under strong control.

The unions also point out that the new technology is not just a crisis for the shopfloor worker. It completely upsets traditional factory hierarchies. Foremen are suffering a crisis of identity under the new automated regimes; upper management, administrators and planners all find that their roles are directly challenged. This is something that the whole of society is going to have to live with.

However, the revolutionary Left returns with a direct challenge: the culmination of this new automation has coincided with the scandal of Fiat's unprecedented sacking of 61 Turin militants, on charges of behaviour not conducive to the well-being of the company. So far from being a social contract with the unions, the restructuring represents a return to the bad old days of the repressive 1950s form of factory fascism. Already posters are appearing on the walls of Fiat-Lingotto announcing THE DUTIES OF THE WORKER. The capitalist restoration is taking place at Fiat, as in the country as a whole. From the capitalist point of view, a highly-automated, computer-controlled factory *must necessarily* be an authoritarian factory, under the full control of the employer. And an authoritarian factory needs an authoritarian society within which to exist.

The history of Ford provides further food for thought. The 1912 introduction of the $5 Day at Ford-USA, accompanied by a new level of mechanisation and factory organisation, was hailed by liberals as a progressive breakthrough. For workers, though, it was the start of a new tyranny, in which, for example, workers were graded into four grades by Ford's morality-inspectors, as to whether or not they were worthy to receive the new bonus. Similarly the announcement of British Leyland's new robot-production plans are virtually simultaneous with the unprecedented sacking of Longbridge convenor Derek Robinson, and with Leyland's announcement that, if the workers do not accept the 1980 pay offer, then BL will impose it over the heads of the shop stewards.

In short, relations between capital and labour have now reached a point of high contradiction. The introduction of new technologies is designed to re-set the balance in favour of capital. Those who support, plan and ease this introduction are seeking to resolve the contradictions in favour of capital. On the other hand, those who wish to see the contradictions resolved in the direction of a radical transformation of society, of power to the working class, seek to block and destroy the implementation of these new automated programmes. Within these terms, today's car worker could argue a very coherent case for Luddism.

* This chapter is a shortened version of an article 'Notes on New Technology and Working Class Resistance in the Motor Industry' shortly to be published in a Red Notes book *A Dossier of Class Struggle in Britain and Abroad: 1978*, ISBN 0 906305 02 0. Available from Red Notes, BP15, 2a St Paul's Road, London N1.

# 10
# Mines

In 1980 the National Coal Board (NCB) intends to introduce a computer control system into 24 pits at a cost of £10 million. The longer term aim is to equip 250 pits with the system, largely by the prophetic year of 1984. The NCB calls this new mine operating system Minos, named after the king of Greek mythology who had a minotaur in his maze of tunnels which he was determined to kill. Is this how the coal bosses see the jobs of the men in the mines? Or, is the NCB's central aim a major improvement in health and safety for miners?

The NCB, the largest mining organisation in the world, is at the forefront of the rapid technological changes taking place in the industry. Many systems developed in British coal mines are exported to other countries, especially those with the type of deep mines that are being worked in Britain. It is likely, therefore, that the way in which the automation of mining is resolved in Britain will directly affect thousands of miners in other countries, from West Germany to China. As with other applications of microelectronics, Minos could cause serious job loss, the degrading of skills and the breakup of present forms of union organisation and pit power.

The technological offensive currently being organised against miners by the Consevative Government is aimed at reducing the present reliance on coal, especially coal mined in Britain. This includes the decision to expand the use of nuclear power in the production of electricity. The Government is in such a rush to do this that it wants to use the American-designed Pressured Water Nuclear Reactor of Three Mile Island infamy, rather than the gas cooled reactor that many reports have indicated is safer. This offensive also includes the decision to spend a lot of money building automated bulk-handling facilities to unload imported coal from bulk carriers. And finally, as the NCB's own intentions emerge from its technical papers, it is becoming clear that there is an offensive underway inside the industry, not only through automation but also by using conventional technology. For example, 300,000 ton bunkers are to be built at Selby to provide emergency stockpiles of coal in case, the NCB would have us believe, there are 'problems on the railways'.

The present attempt to automate mining is not the first. The Remotely Operated Longwall Face failed in the 1960s because, even by 1965, only half of all pits had power loaders and only a quarter had power supports. In addition, the electronic hardware at the time was no match for the tasks involved, although, in theoretical terms, control engineering was well developed.

## Automation of the pit as a whole system

In 1974 the Mining Research and Development Establishment of the NCB carried out a thorough review of research and development work. The objective of automation was presented, again, in terms of automating the whole mining operation. The present attempt is based around new microelectronic technology that has only recently become available. It is a systems-based attempt that is unlikely to fail for technical reasons, as it did in the 1960s. The programme is backed by:

(a) a large annual investment — for example £1.5 million a year just on machine guidance;

(b) 200 electrical and electronic engineers out of a total of 694 research staff in 1978;

(c) the recruitment of specialised staff from the aerospace industry (from Marconi Defence Systems, for example);

(d) the transfer of technology and close collaboration between manufacturers, the NCB and mining management in other countries. The expressed aims of the NCB are to increase productivity greatly, to make considerable labour savings and to increase overall management control.

## Automation of the coal face

Methods of winning coal at the face have changed much in the last 40 years. The backbreaking toil of pick work did not really end until the 1940s. At this time there was a change-over from shortwall coal extraction based on two or three miners acting as a team, to mechanised longwall face working, using production engineering techniques. In the early phase of mechanisation there were considerable problems, as a totally different work organisation was necessary to fit in with the new technology. However, after a period of dislocation, it became apparent that face-workers had become an even more powerful group, since they had immediate command of an increasingly high level of technology. Later came the Anderton

Shearer Loader (ASL), a coal cutting machine, the armoured flexible conveyor (AFC) and hydraulic, powered supports. The ASL was introduced at the coal face in the early 1950s, but was not in widespread use until the mid-'60s. The introduction of shearer loaders and the other two back-up systems at the coal face led to a massive increase in productivity. The average output of a miner increased from 25 cwt. in 1956 to 45 cwt. a shift in 1975.

A typical coal face today will be worked by two or three small teams, each half a dozen strong, on each of three shifts. Each team will be backed up by two to four electricians and fitters. The face team has a high degree of job control—they control the ASL, the AFC and the powered supports, and they can also operate lockouts, a safety procedure that stops all the equipment at the coal face.

At present, there is no one machine that can be used to boost productivity as much as the ASLs did in the 1960s. However, the NCB hopes to achieve a similar boost in productivity using a complete system based on automatic control, automatic information gathering and much improved mechanical and system reliability.

While the attempt to achieve an automated system will be built around the Minos centralised control system, the immediate focus, at the coal face, is the automation of the ASL. At present these machines are manually steered, but from the NCB viewpoint, manual guidance must be replaced by automatic control, so that other equipment at the coal face can also be automatically controlled.

Previous attempts to automate the fixed shearer could not be extended to the more recent ranger type because of the instability inherent in the ranger, and because the analogue electronic hardware was inadequate for steering through three dimensions, or coping with the necessarily sophisticated sensors. Fixed ASLs are now used on only 10% of the coal faces in Britain. Microelectronics has made a timely appearance and a digital system, based on several microcomputers has now been developed to solve the various technical problems. Early in 1979 the first microcomputer-controlled shearer was tried out at Baddesley colliery, Warwickshire. The basic requirement of the automatic ASL is that it must be able to work on 80% of the coal faces, and it must be a stand-alone system that can operate by itself, but that can also be integrated with the AFC, the powered supports and Minos.

*Fido*

A managing microcomputer co-ordinates the work of several other microcomputers that control sensors and other functions. Data is displayed on a display unit on the machine and is also sent to the surface by another part of the system, Face Information Digested On line (Fido). The hardware takes up only 1.3 cubic feet, and is in modular form so that it can be easily replaced for maintenance. The computer programs are designed to instruct the microcomputers to communicate with each other, with data access and display, and to implement machine control; to make calculations on all steering information, store relevant data and send out control signals; to recognise faults and errors and display these at machine, gate – the immediate underground control area near the face – and surface displays. There is also constant monitoring of machine 'health'.

At existing coal faces direct managerial control is exercised by two or three deputies, known either as district deputies or face-end deputies, although, as the NCB safety supervisors in the pits, deputies are supposed to be primarily concerned with safety, rather than with direct supervision. With the introduction of Minos and Fido there will also be a technical form of managerial control, the secondary *management* computer on the surface that, like the main computer, will be linked to every process or machine in the mine, above or below ground.

## The effects of automation on face-workers

What will the automation of the ASL mean for face workers? First, the driver of the ASL will no longer need to stay at the head of the machine in a spray of dust and water, continually exposed to the danger of lung disease, but will be able to stay at the rear. However, exactly what the driver will be doing is not clear from NCB documents. Looking at the software it seems almost certain that the driver and the rest of the face team will face a drastic reduction in both jobs and skill levels. The Department of Employment's *Manpower Implications of Microelectronic Technology* published in 1979, predicts that the typical number of face jobs will be cut from 22 to 15 a shift. This, although serious enough, is likely to be a conservative estimate. The exact implications for skills are not yet clear. What is important to remember, however, is that at present every member of the face team is trained to operate all the equip-- ment at the coal face, although quite often one or two men drive the shearer more than others.

If the present designs are implemented there will be a radical shift in power from the face team to the surface control room, which, where they are already established, are staffed by deputies – members of the supervisors' union (NACODS) rather than the

National Union of Miners (NUM) members. Face workers are in danger of losing their job control as power passes directly to pit managers. Those face workers who remain will be more closely monitored, by technical means as well as by deputies.

What can miners do about this? The application of computers in other industries demonstrates that action is needed quickly, before installation. In the car industry, production workers have demanded that they be taught how to program the robots used for welding or paint-spraying. This leaves job control in the hands of the shop floor rather than transferring it directly to managers or supervisors. Miners will need exact information from the NCB's designers on what they intend the machines to do and what they intend leaving for face-workers to do. Miners could then reject particular proposals, if not the whole system, until a completely different approach is hammered out.

Another question will also need to be looked at, and, like many of the others, it can only be answered by miners themselves – do they want to stay underground? Dust and noise, the danger of explosions and roof falls or possible injury from machinery, all make up a hostile working environment underground. Many people would never work underground, whatever the pay, but for faceworkers the choice is not so simple. Apart from the serious question of job loss, many faceworkers experience positive reasons for staying underground – the camaraderie and solidarity of people working in hostile conditions.

The reverberations of the automation of the face equipment would be felt throughout the NUM where faceworkers hold over 80% of union positions in pit branches, although they make up only 20% of the pit workforce. There can be no doubt that, since the miners' strikes of 1971 and 1974, and the resultant fall of the Heath Government, the Conservatives want miners' power curbed. New technologies have been used to achieve this in many other industrial sectors in the past, from the early days of the industrial revolution to the present. Faceworkers, the militant mass leadership in the NUM and the pit, are in the hot seat once again in the new battle for power.

## Minos

Collieries will be operated under Minos from a central control room installed with a primary minicomputer using a system of microcomputers installed in coal-face machines, coal-clearance and environmental-monitoring equipment, and coal preparation and fixed plant. The primary system is designed for reliability and possible computer failure, while the secondary 'management' computer will collect production information from the coal face and present it to management as well as performance data on the coal clearance system and information for in-depth, long-term analyses. In addition managers will be able to set targets, measure performance, compare results and objectives and apply corrective action. This is close control indeed. Furthermore, the terminals of this secondary system are to be located in management offices only. The system consists of:

(a) Production monitoring: this will provide minute by minute information on, for example, face performance and the cause of delays. One system is working and six others are in development.

(b) Coal clearance: this system was first introduced at Bagworth colliery where 30 conveyor belts and some horizontal bunkers have been automated. The systems are installed elsewhere with many others under development.

(c) Environmental monitoring: this was first installed at Brodsworth colliery with monitoring of nine faces for levels of methane gas, for example. It is in development at six other pits.

(d) Coal preparation: this is installed at Lea Hall colliery. Rawdon colliery has a microcomputer controlled coal preparation operation which is a closed-loop system. This means that computers control the work with workers merely monitoring the process.

(e) Fixed plant.

(f) Management information.

Savings in the cost of labour alone will pay for the Minos controlled coal clearance system within two and a half years. Other subsystems will be quickly paid for by job loss within similar periods.

## Operation

The managing microcomputer installed on the coal face machines, and the others on other parts of the system, are linked to the surface minicomputer in the central control room. Control room operators, members of the supervisors union NACODS or of the NUM, will be unskilled and will need only minimal training. There is a simple push-button command system and colloquial language is used. Configuring is the process of bringing into the operation of the system new parts of the mining operation, so that different parts of the pit can be automated at different times, while following the general systems plan drawn up by the NCB. There are no code tables and the configuring process is protected from outside interference by a progressive set of secret passwords. Power, in this hierarchical, centralised system, lies firmly with the pit managers and engineers.

## Coal preparation

The Minos system also controls the operation of coal preparation plants on the surface. These plants wash and process coal prior to its transportation to, say, power stations. A few small coal preparation plants have already been automated using microelectronics, and another, at South Kirby in Yorkshire, has just been completed at a cost of £18 million. This plant has three computers to regulate its work: one controls coal preparation equipment, one stores and provides managerial information and the other controls the loading of trains for power stations. By 1981 this plant will process 2 million tons of coal from three collieries.

On discovering that the operators of the new plant were to be downgraded and paid less, the NUM branch at South Kirby, backed by the Yorkshire Area Council, has demanded upgrading and more money. Job loss among coal preparation plant operators in nearby pits is likely to be high, as coal is sent straight to the new plant at South Kirby.

The South Kirby plant is a closed-loop system. This is much less skilled work, says the NCB, so the operators will get less pay. The loss of skill, the loss of power and the loss of pay have been designed into the new process plant. How can South Kirby miners grapple with this problem? Most miners feel they should not permanently refuse to operate the multi-million pound plant. If the South Kirby miners win their claim for higher pay and upgrading will this solve their problem? While some particular problems will be solved by this the essential one will remain: management will still have control over the design, development, testing and installation of the system. The new plant has been designed so that management will have very close control of its operation. What demands can be put to change this?

The Minos system, like the automated systems used in other industrial applications, follows some of the worst traditions in process-plant design. Its central aim is the reduction of workers' control over technology and the replacement of this by greatly increased management control. This increased management control is achieved through the deskilling, pacing and monitoring of workers by automatically controlled machinery, a centralised hierarchy of power where traditional top-down forms of management are now built into the technology. Once the system is installed in many pits it will be almost impossible to change its basic design.

There are undoubted safety advantages and improvements inherent in Minos, for if the environmental monitoring subsystem had been installed at Golborne colliery, it is unlikely that there would have been a methane gas explosion and severe loss of life. However, there are clear dangers for miners' job organisation, job security and power at work. Miners should not be afraid to be baited as Luddites if they were to oppose the design of the system, for there are clearly established alternatives in process-plant design in which the role of the human operator is very different.

# 11
# Banking

The last hundred years have been a period of continual growth for British banks. During most of this period they have greatly expanded their branch networks and employed increasing numbers of staff, but the introduction of computer systems in the 1960s marked a decisive break with the past: banks could continue to expand their business but without a corresponding growth in staff. The advent of microelectronic equipment in the 1970s takes this development a stage further since it makes bank growth possible with a reduction in the staff employed. In this chapter we look at the growth of the banking sector since the war, the introduction and extension of automation and the effects on and response of the banks' staff.

## The structure of British banking

Since the nineteenth century there have been great changes in the structure of British banking. Today banking is dominated by only a few banks. This situation developed from the late 1800s when numerous private banks were either taken over or forced out of business by the joint stock banks, which operated as limited companies. Mergers and takeovers left five of them in a dominant position by 1918. These five, who by 1936 accounted for 95% of all banking transactions, were all London clearing banks (LCBs).

In 1968 another spate of mergers resulted in the takeover of some of the smaller LCBs and the big five were reduced to four with the amalgamation of the National Provincial and Westminster Banks to form NatWest. Many of the other clearing banks that exist today are wholly or partly owned by the big four. This concentration enabled the banks to operate a cartel on their interest rate charges until the early 1970s. As a result the banks competed for funds largely by providing services, and in particular by expanding their branch networks. The two features of banking since the war that stand out most clearly are the growth in the banks' business and the increasing competition they have faced from other financial institutions, such as foreign banks operating in this country, finance houses and building societies.

### Automation of accounts

Before the introduction of computers, details of a customer's account and the issuing of statements had to be done by hand in the branch. With the post-war growth in the number of accounts and the number of transactions per account it was necessary for the banks to take on many more staff and expand their branch premises. As early as 1955 the banks had identified records of accounts as an area for automation.

In the late 1950s and early 1960s this automation took place, first by the creation of centralised acccounting and then by introducing mainframe computers in the centres. At first details of transactions were recorded on paper or magnetic tape which then had to be sent to the computer centre for processing. The next stage was to link up a terminal in the branch back office directly with the central computer.

When a transaction is carried out at the counter its details are passed to the terminal operator in the back who then records the details of the transaction. This information is stored in the bank's computer and at the end of each day all the accounts are updated and a statement is produced. The relevant printouts are then dispatched to the branch at which the account is held where they arrive the following morning. This system gives the branch manager almost up-to-date information on the state of the branch customers' accounts.

The effects on staff are difficult to quantify. When computers were first introduced they were expected to lead to a reduction in the number of bank staff but in fact the number increased throughout the 1960s and most of the 1970s. This is explained by the growth in bank business. The introduction of computer systems in the 1960s enabled the growth in staff numbers to be held down.

The main change that occurred in working conditions was a shift from writing figures to keying them into a computer terminal. How these terminals are operated varies between branches. In some, staff alternate between keyboarding and other duties, while in others, staff are employed simply to operate the terminals.

The system described above is known as an offline system because there is only a one-way flow of information from the terminal to the computer and because the accounts are not instantly updated. In an online system, information can also be passed from the central computer to the terminal and accounts can be updated as changes are recorded. To date only a few of the smaller banks have developed online systems—the Trustee Savings Bank has had one since 1971, far longer than any other bank.

In an online system, the terminal is moved from the back office to the teller's counter and is continually linked up to the main computer. For the employers this system has several advantages, despite its relatively high cost. It produces statements that are continously updated, but more important the amount of paperwork is greatly reduced. Details of a transaction are keyed in directly by the teller instead of having to be written down for subsequent processing. The value of a cheque can be directly encoded, rather than being done in a back office, or details of the transaction can be printed on a passbook.

## Cheque clearing

Cash is still the most common way of settling payments but there are also other methods. The most common alternative is a cheque. The use of cheques has grown enormously. It doubled between 1938 and 1964 and trebled between 1964 and 1976, to a total of 1.58 billion. Cheque guarantee cards have encouraged this growth. The quantity of paperwork that has been generated explains why the banks accorded such importance to automatic handling during and after the mid-1950s.

Normally a cheque will be written to someone with either an account at a different bank or at least a different branch of the same bank. If, for example, your groceries are paid for with a Barclay's cheque and the store has an account with Lloyds then a transfer of funds has to be made between the two banks. The system for doing this is called clearing. At the end of a day the total value of Barclays cheques that are payable to accounts at Lloyds is compared with the total value of Lloyds cheques payable to Barclays. The cheques are then exchanged and any difference in value is settled by cash. The same process operates between branches of the same bank.

This process was very labour intensive and time consuming when it was carried out manually. Automation occurred gradually throughout the 1960s. In 1968 developments had reached a point where it was possible to set up an inter-bank computer bureau, later renamed the Bankers Automated Clearing House System (BACS). In 1977 an international clearing organisation was established covering over 500 banks in 15 countries. This is SWIFT, the Society for Worldwide Interbank Financial Telecommunications.

Both BACS and SWIFT rely on being able to read cheques automatically. Since the early 1960s cheques have had the account number and a code that identified the bank and branch printed on them in magnetic ink. At the branch where the cheque is presented the value of the cheque is printed on it as well. The information is read by a machine linked to the computer, which produces tapes for processing by BACS.

The development by the banks of standing order payments and direct debits were further attempts to reduce the volume of paper, and the associated clerical work. They both go further than cheque automation in doing away with the need to process paper at all, except for the initial authorisation.

Standing order payments are generated automatically by the bank's computer which debits the payer's account and again produces a magnetic tape, though this time with details of the credit to the payee's account. This tape is then processed by BACS, as above.

Direct debits are similar to standing orders except that the recipient is able to vary the amount of each payment. Banks only allow large established institutions to do this and they usually have their own computer system. The institution produces a computer tape listing the payer's account details and the amount that is required. They deliver this tape to their own bank which credits their account with the total amount due, then passes the tape to BACS.

Standing Orders and Direct Debits have grown considerably in the 1970s, both between banks and between branches of the same bank. The volume of automated clearings increased by about 14% each year in the period 1972 to 1976.

In summary, the automation of clearing has greatly increased productivity but the effect on staff numbers has been offset by the growth of transactions. In this situation it is easy to see why the banks are pushing ahead with systems of settling payments which can be fully automated.

### Branch reorganisation

In order to reduce the large cost of branches and their staffs, a system known as satellite banking is being introduced. This space-age description conceals an old employers' practice – rationalisation. Traditionally each bank branch has been like a small version of the total bank, providing a whole range of services. Satellite banking would involve taking many of these services away from the individual branch and concentrating them in large area offices. The branches would then effectively become subsidiary to the area office.

For the banks this centralisation of their activities has many advantages. They can concentrate managerial staff in one centre with a full range of expertise. By removing most back office functions from the branches, and by providing a central typing and secretarial service, they can reduce branch staff considerably. Add to that a cash dispenser set in a wall and the reason for the branches' existence collapses.

Midland Bank is committed to this rationalisation and plans to have 37% of its full branches within it by 1982. NatWest is considering a trial run in the Plymouth area some time in 1980. The Co-operative Bank is taking this development a stage further. They do not have a large branch network, and are expanding by providing more bank counters in Co-op shops. At present loans and other back office services are provided by their 64 regional offices, but when their new online computer system is functioning these services will be transferred to it from the regional offices and applications for services will be dealt with by post.

If all of these changes occur, even more branches will be closed than in the late 1970s and the elimination of many senior posts will have serious implications for the career prospects of bank staffs.

## Automated telling

Banks have made a big step towards overcoming their dependence on staff with the development of automatic, through-the-wall cash dispensers. These machines can be situated in branch walls, in railway stations, factories, offices and shops, or anywhere else where they will be secure. They can be used 24 hours a day, seven days a week and do not take holidays or demand better pay and conditions.

The first automatic cash dispensers were introduced in Britain in 1966, and were fairly simple machines only dispensing £10 at a time. They were operated by inserting a special plastic card. After the cash had been dispensed, the dispenser retained the card and a replacement was mailed out from the bank.

Subsequent generations of dispensers, known as Automatic Teller Machines, are much more sophisticated. Like earlier models they are operated by a plastic card but a personal code has to be keyed in as well and the card is returned to the user immediately. Automatic tellers can deliver varying amounts of cash, display the current balance of an account, arrange for a new chequebook or statement to be sent out, and accept cash and cheque deposits.

By late 1979 there were around 1,000 online automatic tellers in Britain, which is roughly half the number in the whole of Europe, though much less than the 15,000 in the USA, and far less than in Japan. The Japanese models even have small printers attached to produce statements and update passbooks, and optical readers to read passbook entries.

The banks feared that there would be consumer resistance, but this does not seem to have occurred to any extent. Indeed, customers have been seen using in-bank dispensers when tellers were free. The introduction of automatic tellers has serious ramifications for bank staffs, so it is not surprising that the bankworkers' union is wary of them.

## Electronic funds transfer

Plans are currently being made to introduce automatic tellers into shops, and in the USA this has already happened. While this does give the shopper the opportunity to obtain cash to pay their bill, it is only one stage on the way to the development of a much more radical system of making payments. This new system involves linking the banks' computers online to an integrated cash-register automatic teller at the checkout known as a Point-of-sale terminal.

A system could work roughly as follows. The cash register would calculate the bill to be paid. The customer would then insert a plastic card into the machine and key in a personal code number. Since it would already have details of the store's account the system could then directly debit the customer's account and credit the store's. This instant transfer of funds by electronics gives the system its name – an Electronic Funds Transfer System (EFT). It clearly has the potential to drastically reduce the volume of paper being cleared and, consequently, many of the staff currently processing it both in central locations and in branches.

In 1980 a full EFT system does not exist but steps are being taken to bring it about. The credit card group, Access, have apparently been vigorously lobbying retailers in order to gain a foot-hold, and in late 1979 a consortium of eleven banks was looking into the possibility of developing a system.

## Bank staff

Three features stand out when looking at the development of bank workers: the growth in absolute numbers, the growth in the percentage of women employed, and the growth of union organisation.

With the growth in bank business and the branch networks there was a corresponding growth in the number of staff and this is particularly evident in the post-war period. In 1949 the London Clearing Banks employed 85,000 staff while in 1974 they employed 206,300. The great majority of these extra workers were women and between the two dates the percentage of women rose from 29% to 57%. Traditionally banking had been a male preserve but during both wars women had to be employed to make up the numbers. After 1918 they were replaced by the returning men, but after 1945 the situation was different. The number of clerical posts increased and with the low level of unemployment in the 1950s and 1960s one of the main attractions of banking as a job, namely the relative security, was eroded.

The banking sector had always been known for its low pay and long hours and there were many more attractive jobs around in the 1950s and 1960s. The banks attempted·to recruit more male staff by breaking with their own traditions and introducing a system of tiered recruitment, dependent on educational qualifications, and this had some success.

Throughout this period trade union membership grew considerably. The National Union of Bank Employees (NUBE) was formed in 1946 and its membership increased as it succeeded in making significant gains for its members.

The question of hours has always been a central feature of the union's policy and throughout the 1970s it has consistently fought to maintain and extend the gains made in the '60s. Three recent examples illustrate this continuing struggle. In 1979 Barclays planned to open a number of *bureaux de changes* with extended opening hours, and the union was successful in insisting that no domestic business be transacted, thus preventing a possible precedent. In the same year the union succeeded in winning the co-operation of Ford shop stewards to black a Midland Bank scheme to open sub-branches with extended opening hours at 22 Ford factories. The introduction of new technology has led to management attempts to open branches for longer since many functions can be handled by the machines, but the union has resisted this as well, for example, by one-day strikes and the blacking of automatic cash dispensers inside a branch.

Hours, however, have not been the only issue. NUBE was only recognised by most of the LCBs after a strike in 1967. The large staff associations in many LCBs present an impediment to the union's objective of creating one union for all workers in the financial sector. A clear illustration of this objective was the change of the union's name in 1979 from NUBE to the Banking, Insurance and Finance Union (BIFU). However the relative weakness of BIFU in the LCBs and the insurance companies may in part explain the ease with which new technologies have been introduced. This may also motivate the banks to automate quickly.

### Major problems for the unions

As the threat to the jobs of bank staffs increases the membership of BIFU has increased from 57,000 in 1967 to 131,000 in 1979. The probability of success in any militant action undertaken by the union is greatly increased once a bank's computer staff is enrolled, since the bank's operation depends on these staff. The 1979 strike action by 500 Midland Bank computer staff resulted in large salary increases for all 200,000 LCB staff, and the threat of action by TSB computer staff later the same year had a similar effect.

Microelectronic equipment will eventually affect all bank staff but the most immediate threat is to the more junior grades who are largely women. Despite formal equality, discrimination against women is widespread in banking and very few women occupy the higher grades. Employers are well aware of the possibility of reducing staff by natural wastage of their women workers. 'There is little hope of getting rid of many career bankers although the high turnover among, especially, female counter staff may have a real impact.' (*TSB Management Review*, January 1980, p. 9.)

Between 1974 and 1976 the number of women employed by the LCBs dropped by 4,800 while the number of men employed increased by 2,200. BIFU is aware of this problem and seems to be making increasing attempts to rectify it by demanding real equality and encouraging women to be actively involved in the union.

At the 1980 BIFU delegate conference a report on microelectronics was overwhelmingly adopted. It takes a very strong stance on new equipment demanding a radical programme of work sharing, including a 28-hour week, and full consultation and negotiation before any more equipment is introduced. These demands are going to be backed by action. This was made perfectly clear by the union's assistant secretary after the conference when he argued that 'unless employers' co-operation was forthcoming his members would refuse to use new word processors or service remote terminals'. (*Computing*, 1 May 1980.)

# 12
# State

A major expansion of the state was a key element in securing the basis for the long economic boom that lasted from 1945 until the early 1970s. Six different elements may be identified in the state's activity during this and the later period. The emphasis accorded to each of these shifted with the growing strength of different sections of the working class.

Right after the war the state intervened in economic reproduction through the Keynesian policy of *demand management*, and in social reproduction through the establishment of the *welfare state*. As these came under increasing strain in the 1960s, the state tried to use first *incorporation* to integrate the trade unions into state institutions and then *compulsion* to discipline union membership. One result of this growing activity has been an expansion of state employment. Transistor-based, and more recently, microelectronic-based computer systems have been important in assisting the management of this activity and in holding down the growth of clerical staff.

Since the late 1960s, increasing emphasis has been given to developing instruments of *repression* to combat rising militancy in Britain and armed struggle in Northern Ireland. Microelectronic technology provides the state with a powerful means of extending the effectiveness of repression.

Finally, the state has increasingly promoted the *restructuring* of industry in an attack on the basis of one of the most concentrated areas of working class power. Microelectronics has been singled out by the state as the main technological means of achieving this.

## *The growth of the state*

The overwhelming electoral victory of the Labour party in 1945 expressed a demand by the working class for fundamental change. The health and educational systems and the other parts of the modern welfare state that were set up then, provided a range of services and a level of security that had never before been available to wide sections of the population. However, the welfare state has tended to reproduce the skills and patterns of authority characteristic of a capitalist society. By relating to members of the working class as individuals, they are separated from the source of their strength, the support and confidence of collective organisation, and so the welfare state contributes to maintaining social stability.

The post-war Labour government also nationalised several major industries, including coal, rail and steel. Each of these was essential to the economy, but years of low investment and long traditions of working-class organisation in each made private capital unwilling to embark on the restructuring that was already overdue, and so this task fell to the state. Many of the new policies had in fact already been proposed during the war by joint committees that included Conservatives.

It was the work of John Maynard Keynes that tried to spell out a strategy for a new period of capitalist development. He provided an ideological justification for a general increase in state activity and proposed specifically that the state should assume responsibility for managing the overall level of demand in the economy, by borrowing if necessary, so that total expenditure would be sufficient to prevent a return to pre-war levels of unemployment.

Orthodox economists maintained that if any commodity could not be sold it was because its price was too high. The cure for unemployment, it followed, was a cut in the real wage. Keynes didn't disagree with this, merely with how to proceed in the face of a highly organised working class, or, as he referred to it, 'the downward rigidity of wages'. His solution was for the state to extend credit so as to promote economic growth, and for part of the higher level of money wages to be recouped through slowly rising prices. Keynesianism was a strategy of planned concession, but its success depended on maintaining control over the level of concessions, so that it didn't backfire and become a strategy for building working-class strength.

As the drawn-out decline of British capitalism became more marked in the 1960s, first Conservative and then Labour governments tried to boost the declining profitability and low growth of the economy by further extending the scale of state activity. Increasingly the main problem was identified as the trade union movement, or more particularly its strong but often unofficial workplace organisation, and at different moments the state tried to use incorporation and compulsion to undermine this power. In 1962 trade union leaders joined representatives of capital and the state on the National Economic Development Council to agree on targets for the growth of wages and other variables. But in 1966 the Labour government resorted to compulsion by introducing a wage freeze; then, in 1967, by doubling unemployment, ended the commitment of post-war governments to full employment. In 1969, the Labour government tried, unsuccessfully, to introduce legal constraints on workers' power. Conservative attempts at compulsion fuelled militancy even more and this was only contained by expanding the state yet further.

## State use of computers

A minor employer before the second world war, by 1950 the state employed nearly 5.8 million people. Throughout the post-war boom, the Keynesian strategy involved conceding, at least partly, to the continual demands for an expansion of the state's welfare services, and, unlike money wages, this could not be clawed back through price rises. Whereas restructuring in the nationalised industries achieved large reductions in the workforce, most other state employment was of a clerical or service nature, which is notoriously immune to attempts to increase productivity. In the ten years to 1976, central and local government employment increased by over 30%.

Until the early 1960s, computers were based on valve technology, and were mainly used for scientific and technical work. The state used them for such applications as census analysis and weapons development. However, during the 1960s, transistor-based computers came to be used much more widely for clerical tasks such as the calculation of payrolls and the control of stock levels. Many of these applications were in local and central state bodies and they limited the growth of clerical labour.

In 1968 the Labour government reorganised the British computer industry by encouraging the merger of four existing manufacturers to form International Computers Limited (ICL). The state was by far the largest customer for computers in Britain and, as well as providing ICL with funds for Research and Development (R & D) and new plant, it established a preferential buying policy that excluded all other suppliers.

As well as being a consumer of electronic technology, state employment also trained workers for the private sector. The Post Office and the Civil Service Department in particular provided extensive technical training for operators, programmers and systems analysts. Only the two biggest suppliers, IBM and ICL, provided the same level of training. Small and medium-sized companies, instead of establishing their own training schemes, poached workers from the state sector by offering higher salaries.

However many of these workers transferred into private industry not only with a technical training, but also with an experience of union organisation. As the structure of employment in Britain shifted away from the male, manual workers who in the past have made up the bulk of trade union membership, the level of unionisation in the expanding state sector has increased.

The fastest growing union in the late 1960s and early '70s was the Association of Scientific, Technical and Managerial Staff which recruited in the private and state sectors. The next three fastest growing unions were the National Union of Public Employees, the National Association of Local Government Officers and the Civil and Public Services Association, all three of which recruited exclusively in the state sector. All have a substantial proportion of women members. By 1976, 85% of State white-collar workers were unionised compared with just 15% in the private sector. Not only have these workers used industrial action to achieve their objectives, but a number of key disputes in the 1970s have occurred in the state sector.

## Substituting computers for clerical workers

The state has made increasing use of computers as they have become cheaper with developments in microelectronic technology. From merely being used to slow down the rate of increase in state employment, computers began to be introduced to actually replace staff. During the 1970s, computers were extended into many new areas so that they became used in nearly every government department. Most government payments are now made by computer. When the Labour government moved to control state expenditure in 1976 through the introduction of cash limits, this was only feasible because a sufficient shift had already occurred towards the computerisation of government financial transactions to enable expenditure to be monitored on a fairly up-to-date basis.

The state had become dependent on the operation of computer systems for its own income from Value Added Tax and an increasing part of its income from direct taxation. This dependence has put the workers who operate the systems in a very powerful position. Post Office workers were the first to take advantage of this by selectively blocking the billing system. The tactic was used more generally by state workers during the 1979 pay dispute with great effect. In November 1979, the Government actually went so far as to try to blame the unusually large 2% rise in the Minimum Lending Rate on the dispute! The state is looking towards more decentralised systems based on mini-computers to overcome this vulnerablility in the future.

Microelectronic technology provides the state with a means of cutting the size of its workforce and of increasing management control over it while overall expenditure is cut. In December 1979, plans were announced to cut 40,000 civil service staff, largely by 1982, at a total saving of £212 million. The computerisation of existing clerical functions was explicitly referred to for many of the departments that are to be affected. Running through the proposals was the general theme that greater productivity could be extracted from fewer clerical workers.

Even before plans to reduce central government employment were announced, the cuts introduced in the mid-1970s by the Labour government had halted the expansion of many local authority offices. Bradford Metropolitan Council, which employs 24,000 workers, including 200 typists in the centre of Bradford, decided early in 1977 to introduce word processors. The pilot scheme cut typing jobs in one directorate from 44 to 22. The other significant changes were that, instead of being spread through various buildings, typists now operating word processors were located in one room in each building for greater supervision; photcopying, reception work and collating, that could be used by typists to break up the monotony of their jobs and create some space for themselves, became specialised activities as a further division of the typing process. Output increased by 19% despite a staff cut of 50%! Greater supervision ensured that error rates per key stroke dropped from one in 59 to one in 367 and the turnaround time of many documents was halved.

## Repression

In the late 1960s the State's policies of incorporation and compulsion became less effective in the face of rising militancy in the UK. Sections of the working class in Ireland resorted to armed struggle; trade unions opposed compulsory regulation; new sections of the working class raised their own demands; and, finally, these developments were paralleled by the rise of an extra-Parliamentary left. Containment was breaking down and the State was unwilling, and increasingly unable, to concede the demands made on it. The repressive aspect of the state policy has been developed and the new technology of microelectronics has proved a useful tool for the organs of State security.

Microelectronics makes extensive surveillance through phone tapping and bugging a much easier task. It also extends the power of State security forces to record and process information on the population. And, finally, it provides much more effective and secure communication between operational units, which increases the effect that a given number of troops and police can have.

International phone, telegraph and telex traffic is monitored by the Government Communications Headquarters (GCHQ) in Cheltenham. To eavesdrop on thousands of phone and telex messages an hour, control stations have been constructed at GCHQ that allow a single surveillance officer to selectively sample the conversations. This automatic tracking of wave bands, indexing and coding of audio messages and selective recording is only possible if it is done semi-automatically under computer control. Cheaper and more reliable components in computers, microelectronics, are essential if GCHQ is to continue its level of surveillance. The amount of computer power necessary to undertake this level of surveillance means that it has only become viable with microelectronic technology. Fault-tolerant computer processors, built of the latest hardware, can switch operations between different circuits and keep going 24 hours a day with the minimum of maintenance. GCHQ is a leader in the use of this type of computer technology and was, for instance, the first UK user of the latest generation of fault-tolerant computer in 1979.

Computer assisted monitoring posts help state security forces tap phone, radio and telex conversations at a tapping centre in the UK.

The domestic phone tapping done by the Post Office at a central site in South London is also dependent on microelectronics. The automatic transcription of speech from a phone into written text is at the contemporary limits of computer technology. Over 1,000 lines can be monitored at the same time with the results going back to military and civil intelligence groups such as MI5 and the Special Branch. High-powered computer systems automatically log calls to and from specified numbers, record the call and, in advance of civil computer technology, print out a transcription from the audio record. The whole set-up was designed by GCHQ for operation by the Post Office and high speed phone lines carry the selected recordings to GCHQ and the state security offices of MI5 and MI6.

With the exchange equipment in use at the end of the 1970s the actual tap was placed on a phone by physically attaching a line to the exchange equipment that controlled the target phone. With the new generation of microelectronic-based exchange, System X, that has been designed for the Post Office by GEC, Plessey and the ITT subsidiary Standard Telephone and Cables, taps can be attached without any physical evidence—it will be possible to monitor phone calls from within the computers that control the System X exchanges.

Apart from these automated methods of gathering information, surveillance of humans by humans remains the major source of information for State security forces. The penetration of groups considered subversive, the collection of information through observation, statements, tax, vehicle, health and other records all produces a mass of data for the security forces to sift. It is through the process of sifting and collation that this raw data becomes meaningful information about the movements, activities and allegiances of the individuals whom the State security forces have identified as targets.

The correlation and processing of this data can only be achieved with the introduction of cheaper computer processing power and mass storage. Three projects in the UK, each of them based on computers, have enabled security forces to extend their powers in the last five years.

First, in Northern Ireland computers located in Lisburn and run by the British Army have been systematically fed with data from informers, foot patrols, the results of interrogations and other sources. A detailed pattern of information on the life of individual citizens has been established to the point where the internal layout and decorations of the houses of a sizeable number of the population is available for cross checking and correlation.

Secondly, a pilot project for the Thames Valley Police Force has put what the police call criminal intelligence onto Honeywell computers so that their individual police stations can retrieve it. The data held on the system includes rumour, conjecture and circumstantial evidence on the population policed by the force. Large sections in the files which cover about a third of the total population in the area, are kept for comments that can be entered without the person entering the data being identified. This information can then be manipulated, browsed through, matched against the circumstances of a crime or any other event, and the results forwarded to computer terminals in the stations from which, over radio links, they are available within seconds to the force on patrol.

Thirdly, at Scotland Yard, a complex network of minicomputers has been established to computerise the files of the Special Branch, the Drug Squad, the criminal intelligence unit, CII, and the immigration unit. Each service can only access its own data—apart from the Special Branch, which can range over the whole database. The system went live in May 1979 and is kept up to date just like an ordinary filing cabinet by the four users. As with the Thames Valley system, security services can browse through it looking for matching data or put questions to the system which will prompt an automatic search. The example given by Scotland Yard of the type of data the system can automatically retrieve was 'List all the red-headed Irish men driving white Cortina cars in the London area'. The answer to this type of query is available within seconds.

Finally, the most complex application and one that the security forces have been least successful in developing is a computer-assisted system to control patrols from central command posts. These systems are being extensively used to monitor traffic in most big cities but the complexity of keeping track of thousands of police and police vehicles in London alone has, so far, proved too much. Technically it is not a big task—it is just that the volume of computer processing power and high speed storage that is necessary is, at the beginning of the 1980s, prohibitively expensive. But the falling price and increased speed of microelectronics must soon bring this application within the increased budget of the police.

The British Army has been deployed more and more within the UK. As well as the 'action in support of the civil powers' in Northern Ireland, the Army has been active in breaking public service strikes and has set up combined operations with the civilian authorities in most large centres of population. In 1978 just over 40% of the budget for the Ministry of Defence was spent on operations and maintenance, with personnel costs of £1.6 billion accounting for

22%. Expenditure on new equipment accounted for 23%, split between £1.2 billion on air systems, £601 million on land systems, £878 million on naval systems and £291 million on 'others'. A large amount of this expenditure on equipment was for weapons and communiations systems that include a high proportion of micro-electronics. Within the budget for the armed forces, which has been increased despite the planned cut in total government expenditure announced by the Conservative Government in 1980, a much higher proportion has been allocated in the coming years for the purchase of equipment. From the 23% in 1978 it will rise to 40% in the fiscal year 1980-81, almost doubling to a total equipment budget of £4.3 billion. Some of this equipment will undoubtedly be used to extend the role of the armed forces in domestic security operations. Whatever its use, it all adds up to a massive rearmament programme. The effects of rearmament are not only in the 'international' sphere — they also extend the power that the military exercises within its own country.

## Restructuring

With the shift away from the Keynesian policies of demand management and welfare expenditure, increasing emphasis has been placed on restructuring the industrial base where a crucial source of working-class power is concentrated. State intervention in industry was extended by the 1974-79 Labour Government. The policy of non-intervention publicly advocated by the 1979 Conservative government should not be taken to mean that this direct restructuring under the guidance of the State has been abandoned; it has become more selective and is taking up a greater proportion of a decreased budget to support and extend the role of microelectronic technology.

Some restructuring was achieved during the mid-'70s through nationalisation, for instance in the shipbuilding, aerospace and motor industries, but in the main, new forms of direct intervention were developed from the mid-1960s onwards — intervention which didn't challenge private ownership and which tried to strip the economic relationships directly under the command of the State of any political content by reintroducing commercial criteria.

The Ministry of Technology was formed by the Labour Government in 1964 with the explicit responsibility of encouraging private capital to introduce the four key technologies of computers, electronics, telecommunications and machine tools into production processes. It grew rapidly to assume overall responsibility for industrial policy, and under the Heath government in the early

1970s it became the Department of Industry. After the famous U-turn, the Department was given extensive powers for selective and regional intervention under the 1972 Industry Act.

By the time Labour regained Parliamentary power micro-electronics had come to the forefront of the new technologies. The Department of Industry, the Department of Education and Science and the newly established National Enterprise Board were used to nurture this new and potentially profitable sector of industry and to urge other industries to use microelectronics in their own production processes.

The National Enterprise Board (NEB) emerged out of the proposals the Labour Party had developed in opposition during the Heath Government when an old left, centred on the Tribune Group, gave way to a new left associated with Stuart Holland and Tony Benn who argued for an industrial policy as an alternative to the discredited use of compulsion. The defeat of 'In Place of Strife', the influx of students and ex-students that shifted the Labour Party leftwards, and the strength of the organised sections of the working class gained by defeating the Heath Government, forced the new Labour Government to make huge concessions in its first six months. In 1974 the Labour leadership needed a policy that could head off the left's strategy. The Labour Government's white paper on industrial strategy therefore proposed planning agreements – that were used in the sole case of Chrysler – industrial democracy which was diffused by the setting up of the Bullock Commission and then shelved – and the National Enterprise Board (NEB) – that would act both as a holding company and as a source of funds. The left saw the NEB as an umbrella for holding a major company in each industrial sector as a move towards a fundmental shift in wealth and power. Existing holdings in 'lame duck' companies were transferred from the Department of Industry. Then small but profitable and growing concerns, more often than not involved in the microelectronic industry and software production, became the target for minority shareholdings. These shareholdings were outside democratic control so reducing the appearance of economic relations to a technical relationship by reintroducing commercial criteria into the relation between the State and private capital. The NEB is required to get a rate of return on its investments equal to the average in private industry.

The NEB staged a strategic review of industrial production and developed a plan to overcome the weakness of the UK software industry in the international market. None of the big software packages used by computer users in the West were written in the

UK, but were all supplied, with one exception, from the US. An organisation, Insac, was established both as a means of breaking into the world software market and as a means of providing venture capital to software houses like Computer Analysts and Programmers, systems houses, like Systime, and broadly based computer service companies like Logica. Through the latter end of 1976 and the whole of 1977, NEB funds bought between 20% and 35% of six of the fastest growing UK computer companies and acted on their Boards with the discretion of a private merchant bank.

Each of the six had an expertise in some crucial area like programming process control computers, building business systems on US-made mini processors by adding more hardware and software, developing software for microprocessor-based systems, and writing the software for word processors.

In this initial period little, if anything, was done to develop any serious international marketing strategy for the products of these companies. Instead, in late 1979 the US marketing arm of a software company in which the NEB had no stake was taken over to provide the marketing force.

The biggest international operation came with the establishment of Inmos, the venture to build microelectronic memories and processors in the UK and the US centred on two leading engineers in the US from the pioneers in microelectronic memory, Mostek, and a UK industrial figure. An initial investment of £25 million was put into Inmos to build plants in the US and the UK, with another £25 million promised on results.

The business planners in the NEB had gained their experience in merchant banking rather than in industrial management or the labour movement. After the formation of Inmos they turned their attention to a major area of applications for microelectronics – office automation. Senior managers were recruited from IBM to head the Nexos venture that would first market word processors and facsimile machines and then develop its own office systems by developing electronic message switching and other components for the fully automated office.

Once Insac members had received the initial venture capital and found that little was being done about the international marketing of their products, the political climate had changed with the Conservative victory of 1979 and they became more forthright in their criticisms. The originators of the Insac scheme within the NEB either left or switched their focus to what seemed the more profitable area of selling products for viewdata systems by forming Insac Viewdata, which later emphasised its separateness by dubbing itself Aragon.

Throughout the whole period the Department of Industry (DoI) continued to be a major source of funds for R & D capital expenditure. Industry is urged to apply microelectronic technology through the Microprocessor Applications Project backed by £25 million State funds. Added to the £50 million going to Inmos, the joint venture between GEC and Fairchild received state aid as did the expansion of plants in the UK by US manufactures such as Motorola, Texas Instruments and National Semiconductor.

Funds for R & D by the Department of Industry were channelled through the Computer Systems and Electronics Requirements Board. Just under £9 million was spent by the Board in 1977-78, which was 7.2% of the total gross expenditure on R & D by the DoI. This was raised to 10.3% in 1078-79 to stand at £13.7 million. At the same time many of the other efforts at R & D funded by the DoI were urged to take up microelectronic applications so that the total of microelectronics R & D supported by the DoI was far in excess of this single Board's expenditure.

Another major source of funds was the Department of Education and Science which, during the late 1970s, switched its emphasis from funding big science projects to projects which had a more direct industrial application such as, yet again, the application of microelectronics.

The R & D that resulted in the only microprocessor designed and manufactured in Western Europe, the Ferranti F100L, was largely funded by the Ministry of Defence in the late 1970s. This commitment to basic electronics R & D was emphasised by the plans to spend £1.1 billion in 1980-81 on R & D, much of which will be channelled to the biggest microelectronic based industrial suppliers such as GEC, Ferranti, Plessey, EMI, Racal, Sperry, Philips, Decca, Mullard and Standard and Telephone, in that order.

## Other State Strategies

The strategy a state adopts over the development and use of microelectronics depends on the strength of any existing microelectronic industry within that country, the place that nation holds in the capitalist world market and the current policies being adopted by the ruling group.

Where the state is trying to defend the national industry against foreign competition, then a mixture of import controls, preferential purchase policies, direct funding of R & D and aids to the formation of capital will be adopted. Without a national industry to defend, states adopt policies aimed at aiding capital from outside their borders which, with the domination of US capital in the world microelectronic industry, means US-owned multinationals.

France, for instance, adopted a policy of state support in which three major US multinationals played key roles in a co-ordinated attempt to develop French industry. The same is true of Italy which, as well as direct support for indigenous capital and joint ventures, put great emphasis on the state as a customer by boosting the demand for microelectronic-based products in central and local government.

The Irish state, on the other hand, adopted a classic policy of enticing foreign capital as a tax haven with pre-built factories, capital grants and rent rebates. Since the late 1960s Japan has adopted the full range of policies, including punitive import duties, aimed at defending the Japanese electronics industry while it is restructured into a microelectronics industry that can operate successfully in the world market. The results of Japan's policy have been significant because, while production of microelectronic-based goods has rapidly expanded, imports have remained steady and exports have risen ten-fold in just over a decade.

# 13
# Education

This chapter introduces some of the issues concerned with the *content* of the education available to adults, to school students and in higher education. This inevitably touches on the *form* of that education. Finally, it raises some questions on the complex relationship between microelectronics, education and the process of social change.

The role of education in the reproduction of a disciplined workforce, the role and location of new technology in the curriculum, the links between education and industry and the changes in the labour process within education are all mentioned here; however, they are only a small selection. This chapter is not intended to be an exhaustive survey.

## Mystification

Discussion of the impact of microelectronics, like debates on nuclear energy or the siting of the third London airport, are extremely inaccessible to the very people whose lives are affected by their outcome. The media rarely provide unbiased reporting; independent assessment of a television documentary programme or any newspaper article is impossible. People feel that informed opinion on technological issues is the preserve of 'the experts' and that they are ill-equipped for the task of challenging what has been said.

Such mystification has been particularly noticeable on the topic of computers, linked as they are to the 'big brother' model of social control. The misplaced humanisation of powerful machines – 'the computer must have made a mistake, Sir' – and jokes about computers sending each other cheques for £00.00p, all of which were meant for reassurance, have merely confused everyone further. Thus, it is hardly surprising that new developments in computing that affect more people, more closely, are the subject of the same puzzlement.

## *Adult education*

Traditionally, evening classes were the place to go to try to fill in the gaps in an individual's education. So far, only a few institutes have managed to find the resources to staff and run courses on micro-electronics. Hopefully, their numbers will increase because of the importance of the issue, but the financial cuts imposed on local education authorities by the Tory government that was elected in May, 1979 hit adult education provision very severely, closing all classes in at least one authority and raising fees everywhere. Not only is the prospect of basic informational courses dwindling, but every non-vocational evening class, from Local History to Weaving, is threatened. All may soon be driven out of existence, thus annihilating the somewhat utopian and outdated notion of 'education for leisure'.

The only alternative source of courses for adults on micro-electronics may stem from trade union education, currently an expanding area. The Trades Union Congress Education Programme on New Technology supports the local branches of individual unions in setting up their own short courses for members. It also sponsors a number of two- to five-day specialist short courses for union members and full time officials and emphasises the need for discussion of new technology in existing short courses; Health and Safety courses, for example, should include a session on the hazards of visual display units. Sadly, such well-intentioned efforts are likely to be available to only a small proportion of trades unionists. Further, they are totally inacessible to people outside the trade union movement, especially housewives and the unemployed.

## *Studying by correspondence*

Another possibility is to study at home with the National Extension College, a correspondence college run commercially as an educational trust. Its TV course 'The Silicon Factor: Living With The Microprocessor' is advertised as: 'A study pack to help you look at what the silicon chip might do to our society'. It is wide-ranging and lucidly written, with three accompanying programmes on BBC2. The cost of £1.50 is acceptably low, but this particular method of studying can only provide a cheap, isolated substitute for class teaching and group discussion.

At the other end of the spectrum is the new short course from the Open University: 'Microprocessors and Product Development: A course for Industry'. This is 'designed to give managers and decision-makers in industry an understanding of how the process of development of a product is affected by the introduction of a micro-processor'. Clearly, a course for those well on the way to being 'experts' themselves, put further out reach for the ordinary person by the £120 course fee. A second similar course, scheduled for 1981, will be aimed at engineers.

A feature of both the TUC Programme and the Open University courses' is the way in which they are financed by government funds channelled via the Department of Industry's Microprocessor Application Project (MAP). This is designed specifically to provide education about microprocessors for skilled personnel – engineers and technicians – thereby limiting, for those funded, the scope to produce courses with a wider appeal and market. However, other colleges and educational institutions are now tapping this source in order to finance and retain courses and increase their student numbers in a vocational area that might otherwise have suffered from the cuts. Thus, MAP is providing a useful alternative source of public funds for education, despite the changes in the courses required to fulfill MAP criteria.

## Computer education in secondary schools

If we are gloomy about the provision of courses on microelectronics for adults, we might reasonably hope that the prospects for school students are brighter. Surely they, at least, must be learning about the latest technological revolution which, it is said, will have such a profound effect on their adult lives?

But the picture, yet again, is piecemeal, revealing a total lack of coherent planning. New subjects establish their place in the curriculum slowly and painfully. Throughout the 1970s the fate of Computer Studies in secondary schools in England and Wales usually depended on the level of enthusiasm of Mathematics teachers. If they were active and could persuade their Heads to finance the purchase of an expensive mini-computer (more likely in a public school) or the processing of programs at a local firm or college (more likely elsewhere), then the subject survived. If they were not interested, it never got going at all. Very few local education authorities have Computing Advisers; few schools have specialists appointed to teach the subject. Nevertheless it remained a growth area, to the point where, in 1976, the numbers of pupils taking O and A levels was high enough for the subject to merit a separate entry in the Department of Education and Science's statistics. There is also now at least one A level syllabus in Electronics, another closely related subject of growing popularity.

*Table 13.1:* Figures for pupils taking computer subjects at O and A level.

|  |  | No. of pupils entered | |
|  |  | Boys | Girls |
| O level: Computer Studies | 1976 | 2,359 | 829 |
|  | 1977 | 4,593 | 1,701 |
| A level: Computer Science | 1976 | 1,218 | 328 |
|  | 1977 | 1,441 | 429 |

Source: *Statistics in Education*, HMSO

These figures, of a small elite group, serve to illustrate the phenomenon of low numbers of girls taking science and technology subjects in schools. The statistics on Certificate of Secondary Education entries do not yet show Computer Studies separately, although many schools offer their own syllabus in the subject.

In Scotland, where the Scottish Education Department operates a unified approach throughout the country to most aspects of education, a more coherent picture emerges. For the last 10 years nearly all secondary schools have had terminal or postal access to computing facilities established at educational computer centres attached to the six major colleges of education. Further, all graduate teachers trained at these colleges have some computing component built into their courses. These measures, taken together, ensure that Computer Studies is at least a feasible option in most Scottish secondary schools, whereas, in England and Wales, a universal pre-service computing syllabus for student teachers has only recently been proposed.

At a more general level, the social aspects of computing tended to be glossed over everywhere, mainly because Computer Studies was taught as a technical subject by specialists in other subjects. Often, schools or teachers' centres bought a teaching package on computers, hoping that teachers would use it with lower ability groups. These packages came from the manufacturers, as with ICL's 'Computer Education in Schools', or from centrally funded bodies such as the National Computing Centre's 'Computers and their impact on Business and Society' and the Schools Council Project 'Computers in the Curriculum'. Some computer manufacturers, notably IBM, ran an Information and Advisory Service for schools and still others ran special users' groups for educational purchasers of their equipment. In some parts of the country, manufacturers 'adopted' schools in order to develop closer links with them. Quite who benefits from these activities, the schools or the manufacturers, is open to debate. Pupils who first learn the specialist terminology of a particular range of equipment, and are then told of the progressive applications of that same equipment (by an apparently benevolent, open-minded multi-national!) are unlikely to change their loyalty when they become adult members of the workforce. The supposedly free market for computer equipment can, in part, be skillfully manipulated and cornered by an unsubtle process of early conditioning.

Gradually, though, as more and more schools are able to afford the cheaper microcomputers, teaching about them is broadening out. More teachers are aware of the need for their pupils to study them, and they are also realising their potential as a tool in teaching other subjects, such as Geography and Economics. At the level of state policy, even the recent discussion paper on the curriculum recognised the need for schools to respond to 'new needs as they are identified and new knowledge as it emerges ... they have to consider the advent of microelectronics and the wider social and industrial consequences of new technology'. Despite this official acknowledgement, there is no plan in Britain, as there is in France, to equip all secondary schools with microcomputers, even as part of the move to standardise the curriculum; currently only 200 out of 6,000 schools are reported to have them (*New Scientist*, 11 January 1979), although many more do have terminals giving them access to larger machines.

In March 1979, under a Labour government, the Department of Education and Science (DES) announced its intention to spend £12.5 million on a five-year programme administered by the Council for Educational Technology, 'to help schools and colleges become aware of the wider implications of microeletronics and to help them make the best use of the opportunities it offers' (*Computer Education*, June 1979). Following the election victory of the Conservatives in May 1979 this, like other current and proposed education expenditure, came under review; exactly a year later a figure of £9 million was specified, a 25% cut. It will be some time before precise details of the DES spending plans materialise, although it is already clear that the money is not to be used for purchasing equipment which must be charged to other local education authority budgets (*Guardian*, 5 March 1980). In the meantime, it may be worth considering the questions: What opportunities? For whom? To quote from the document itself:

The programme will be concerned primarily with the applications of the new technology rather than with its science. It will not cover specialist training in microelectronics, for which arrangements are being studied separately, since neither the schools nor the majority of further education courses need to be concerned with how microprocessors are made or the detail of how they work. The programme will of course help indirectly by contributing to a foundation of good school science courses including electronics and ready access to computing facilities. Nor will it be concerned with promoting studies of the wider, long-term implications of microelectronics for society—for example, on employment and leisure patterns or on re-training and the general provision of adult education. (DES, *Microelectronics in Education: a development programme for Schools and Colleges*, HMSO, 1979, paragraph 7).

Curriculum development, teacher training facilities, an extended computer assisted learning study and the development of links between educational institutions and local electronics industries are all mentioned specifically. The overall focus and intention, however, is quite explicitly to embrace new technology and ensure that children and young people are prepared to be versatile and adaptable in adult life, participating in a changed labour process with ease.

The Department of Industry Microprocessor Application Project money has also funded educational research projects, such as the Investigation on Teaching with Microcomputers as an Aid (ITMA) based at a college in Plymouth (*Computer Education*, June 1979). Here again, the interests of industry and education are seen as closely intertwined, with many of the activities proposed having a direct input to or output from local industry.

## *Primary schools*

There is no doubt that younger children growing up in an age when electronic toys and games are available for home purchase, at an ever lower price, or in amusement arcades, will treat microelectronics as a fact of life. In primary schools, microcomputers, which are still beyond the scope of most equipment budgets, would not be at all out of place. They could provide opportunities for innovation in teaching and flexibility in learning for individual children, allowing each child to work at its own pace on projects it alone enjoys.

This said, the situation must not be allowed to develop in which new technology in the classroom is used to increase the size of classes, to transform teachers into childminders or to reduce the occasions for individual, personal contact between adults and children. Passive submission to a visual display unit should not provide the keynote for future discipline, or set the pattern for social control. Nor must this be used as an opportunity to take a reductionist, quantified approach to every aspect of the curriculum, which would make everything that a child does subject to formal assessment and examination. The dangers of overemphasising intellectual skills to the detriment of emotional development cannot be ignored.

Even when computers are part of the school curriculum, the social aspects are glossed over since it is taught as a technical subject.

### Education administration

School clerks and secretaries are reported by one local branch of the National Association of Local Government Officers to be amongst those members most firmly opposed to the introduction of new technology. This is probably because their pay is low and they are completely isolated from their colleagues doing similar work in other schools. Their position is very vulnerable; they are aware of the need to resist pressures to remove their control over their work.

Yet computer enthusiasts amongst the teachers wax lyrical over the computerisation of administrative tasks in large schools, little realising or caring that jobs of other school workers are thereby threatened (see, for example, R. Green, 'Administration on a school microprocessor?' *Computer Education*, November 1979). It may be that there are grounds for developing solidarity between different categories of workers in schools, especially in the current climate of financial stringency.

In colleges and universities, however, where secretarial and clerical staff are increasingly operating word processors, the situation seems to differ slightly. Since boss/worker relationships are often more cordial, at least superficially, and departmental offices are small and closely knit, the acquisition of the new technology has sometimes been welcomed. Indeed, these may be some of the few offices where there is consultation between management and workers *before* the equipment appears, where workers are able to retain control over their jobs and the rhythm of their day, and where, despite the long term threat to their jobs, they are able to regard new equipment as bringing them status over other, non-automated departmental offices. (In most further and higher education institutions many of the administrative functions such as budgeting, purchasing, holding student records and scheduling examinations have long been centralised and automated using a mainframe college computer.)

In the face of public spending cuts, however, it seems likely that this unusual atmosphere of co-operation will diminish, as word processors are systematically introduced in the name of efficiency to cut the cost of living labour power. (See chapter 5 for a more detailed description of the impact of microelectronics on office work).

## Micros in the universities

Whereas some university and college departments are struggling to maintain their viability in the face of the spending cuts, those offering undergraduate and postgraduate courses in Computer Science, Electronics or Engineering Design are booming. Microprocessors have changed both the content and the teaching methods in all these subjects. Because these departments are able to attract students, they are also able to argue for a sizeable share of the scarce financial resources to buy new equipment.

In other subject areas, microprocessors are increasingly viewed as a powerful teaching tool, useful, particularly for design exercises (Architecture, Civil Engineering), gaming simulation (Business Studies, International Relations) and modelling (Biology, Economics).

Academic research, in general, funded sparsely from currently low educational resources, is also boosted where microprocessors and their applications are involved. Yet again, private and public industry, those generous benefactors, pour money into the education sector and confidently expect to gain from the outcome. Many universities are conducting applied research which, for example, will refine the use of robots on production lines. Others have set up their own commercially run microelectronics consultancy centres, either independently or hand-in-hand with local industry, offering advice or courses, as appropriate, and spreading expertise to the inexperienced. The income from such activities goes some way towards cushioning applied science and technology in higher education from the effects of government measures such as raising overseas student fees.

## Perspectives

While it is obviously necessary to fight for the inclusion of courses on new technology at all levels of the education system, so that all adults and children understand the changes that are taking place around them, it is also important to recognise the bias in public sector education which protects the dominant capitalist ideology. Within this, there is an interest in perpetuating existing class and sex divisions in society. Schools have so far concentrated most of their efforts on specialist teaching in computer education, producing entrants for O and A level examinations (see Table 13.1); these are the high-fliers, the skilled elite who will go into higher education and become the next generation of technicians and engineers — tomorrow's 'experts'. For the rest, most of whom are likely to find themselves joining the millions of unemployed because their future jobs have already been automated by new technology, lower standards and less effort are acceptable. Docile compliance and a consumption oriented value system would not be characteristic of a workless population educated to think and understand technology of any kind. Nor is it illogical that politicians of all parties go to great lengths to encourage links between industry and education, but assert in their next breath that technology is politically and ideologically neutral and value-free. It is an easy matter to agree to teach a course on new technology, but very difficult to design a syllabus that explains what it is and how it can be used without appearing to accept its introduction uncritically. There must be room for open discussion in all courses, and the dangers and threats to jobs, to health and to accessibility of personal information must be made explicit.

Teachers, taking their lead from the TUC, have responded to government initiatives by embracing new technology and all that it represents. So far, discussion within the main unions has centred on the need to incorporate the idea of increased opportunities offered by brave new technological progress, and they deplore only the lack of funds that prevents them from implementing instant change in the classroom. When teachers themselves finally feel threatened by deskilling, open discussion within the educational profession will become crucial. On the whole, educational technology has always been welcomed by the teaching unions, but this attitude could justifiably change if teaching skills were transferred to microcomputers, making some teachers superfluous in the classroom and finally redundant. Were they about to suffer the same fate as their pupils, teachers might well subvert and change the educational process and the inequalities it sustains.

# 14
# Training

To workers, training is a means of developing a set of skills that can be used to increase their wage and perhaps, give them a little more satisfaction in their wage labour. To the employers, training is a problem because workers with skills can change jobs if those skills are in demand, and the skills give the worker more control over production. Companies generally take a short-term view of training and are less reluctant to provide upgrading training for existing workers or to recruit trainees when their order books are full and their demand for skilled labour is high.

A new technology demands a new set of skills to go with it. Education can equip workers with the skills necessary to tackle unpredictable events in the use of the technology. Training, however, aims to give workers only that knowledge which they need to slot them into a particular, restricted place in the production process.

Despite the calls for the adoption and application of micro-electronics in British industry issued by the government, little fundamental education has been established in basic microelectronic technology. There is, instead, a coherent strategy to develop certain skills in the work force that will be essential to the further application of microelectronics.

This strategy goes hand in hand, rather than contradicting, a programme of cuts in education. Training for skills related to micro-electronics is getting an increased share of a declining state budget for training. And the state has developed a central role in the provision of training in the last thirty years as managements have taken the short term view and cut training provisions as one of their methods of keeping up profits.

In trying to fill the training gap, the state has adopted three strategies since the end of World War II. Firstly it provided Government Training Centres in which to rehabilitate disabled servicemen. Then the Centres changed their role to providing training during periods of unemployment to fill gaps on the labour market. The second strategy was to attempt to encourage an expansion of the training provided in industry. This strategy was dominant in the period from 1964 to 1973. Then, as the British economy entered its present phase of restructuring, the state took a more direct role in providing training by restructuring the education offered in further education in line with demands of the job market.

As the third strategy unfolded, orchestrated by the Manpower Services Commission, microelectronics emerged as the most important technology in the period of reconstruction and training for microelectronics took up a front position in the priority list. This chapter deals with those three strategies, the response they evoked from management and organised labour, and the sections of the working class, such as women, who have been excluded from the strategy.

## Government training centres

In the late 1950s, when the electorate was being told that they had never had it so good, Government reports were pointing out that other countries were having it better. A major cause of the com-paratively poor growth in the UK as against the growth in West Germany was alleged to be a shortage of skilled workers. It was plain that industry was not training sufficient workers but a 1958 inquiry concluded that a radical increase in state involvement would distort the picture and the private sector should be left to its own devices.

For the previous thirty years the state's main involvement was the training of ex-servicemen and disabled persons in Government Training Centres. From 1963 on this social role was replaced by an economic role aimed at training unemployed and non-skilled workers in surroundings resembling factories in skills for which there was a strong demand.

The Government Training Centres produced workers who, after six months to a year's training, could undertake a limited range of skilled tasks. Shop floors generally strongly resisted the introduction of these 'dilutee' tradesmen and they were placed in a weaker position than other workers in times of redundancy or layoffs.

## Providing incentives to train

As the difference between Britain's comparatively low economic growth and the expansion in the rest of the world capitalist economy became more marked in the early 1960s, the Conservative Government set out to reorganise the training efforts of industry and the state by establishing Industrial Training Boards covering

industries employing about half of the workforce. The members o
the Boards were drawn 'from both sides of industry', so 'incor
porating trade union officials. The Training Centres were not given
prominent position in this reorganisation and most unions officiall
backed the Boards as they felt that national standards of trainin
could be enforced that would not dilute the basis of skills in th
workforce.

A major aim of the Boards was to increase the quality an
quantity of training undertaken within individual companies
Companies within the industry covered by the Board paid a lev
calculated as a tax on the payroll and received grants financed by th
levy for their own training. This grant-levy system was supposed t
place a toll on companies poaching trained workers from their rivals

The Boards mainly covered the traditional male preserves o
manufacturing but there were also Boards for distribution, hotel an
catering industries that have a high proportion of women workers
Most of the commercial sector and local government employmen
was, however, excluded. The functions of the Boards continue
under the Labour Governments of the late 1960s and early 1970s.

### Turning education into training

In the period up to the mid-1970s the two policies of direct trainin
and the co-ordination of industrial training through Training Board
were adopted, with the emphasis on the latter policy. As the Britis
economy went through the slump of 1973/4 that ended the post
war boom, the policy for training was re-examined and, through th
1970s, a coherent strategy emerged to cut education and replace i
with vocational training.

Employers resented the imposition of the levy by the Boards an
claimed that it restricted their ability to decide what was best fo
their own need. In 1973 the role of the Boards was reduced whe
their powers to collect the levy were cut back to the point that som
of the smaller Boards gave up collecting the levy at all. At the sam
time the Manpower Services Commission (MSC) was established
despite the objections of trade unions who feared a return to th
Government Training Centre mentality.

The MSC was to be an umbrella organisation covering all aspect
of manpower policy. It had two sections: one aimed at placin
workers in employment through Jobcentres and the other wa
responsible for training. Training covered the old Training Boards, a
well as the directly controlled Training Opportunities Scheme (Tops
and the Training Centres that were renamed Skillcentres. The Tops

programmes provided funds for courses not only in Skillcentres but also in colleges of further education, thus tying a third part of the training effort directly into state policy.

The MSC got into its stride at the same time as the Government began to cut funds to education. As the recession deepened after 1974, the MSC shifted its priority towards dealing with the unemployed.

The range of Special Programmes that were developed, especially after 1975, to cope with increasing unemployment grew to such an extent that they were hived off from the Training section to form a separate division of the MSC in 1978.

While non-vocational education was being axed in the Labour Government cuts of the late 1970s, the state-directed effort to train workers in skills for industrial work grew. In 1973 the MSC spent £125 million funding its various activities; by 1978 this had grown to £630 million.

Under the cuts announced in the opening months of the Conservative Government during 1979, the emphasis of the work of the MSC was shifted again — this time microelectronic skills were given priority with expanded funds while the rest of the MSC's budget was cut back to a projected £360 million in 1980-81.

Training opportunities that were particularly affected by this round of cuts fell most heavily on women. During 1978 and 1979, for instance, women took up nine out of ten places for training in clerical and commercial skills as opposed to an average of four out of ten overall. And it was clerical and commercial subjects that were most severely cut back at the same time that microelectronic training was boosted.

*Table 14.1* Men and women completing state provided training in 1978/79.

| Type of course | Women Number | % | Men Number | % |
|---|---|---|---|---|
| Clerical and commercial | 22,156 | 91 | 2,162 | 9 |
| Management | 1,208 | 19 | 5,110 | 81 |
| Seience and Technology | 94 | 9 | 900 | 91 |
| Craft skills | 314 | 1 | 28,228 | 99 |
| All courses | 28,332 | 40 | 42,033 | 60 |

Source: Hansard, 1979.

The MSC spends a lot of its time trying to defuse the dissatisfaction of young people who find it increasingly difficult to get work. From January 1972 to January 1977 the number of unemployed 16 to 17-year-olds in the UK rose by 120% compared with a 45% rise in total unemployment. The state is concerned over three aspects of youth unemployment. First, it fears the political and social unrest that may be caused. Secondly, it fears that a large section of a whole generation may become unemployable because it will have had little experience of work discipline. Finally it fears that a future upturn in the economy will leave industry short of crucial skills, thus crippling growth in a rerun of the events of the 1950s.

The MSC has turned to the existing institutions of education. Technical and Further Education Colleges, and through special programmes funded courses built around MSC-approved syllabuses. The expansion of these programmes, often considered a mere device to keep down unemployment figures, has happened at the same time as general cuts in education. The influence of the MSC and its vocational-oriented courses has therefore increased in Colleges to the point where the Department of Education and Science is concerned over losing control of Colleges. Teaching institutions that have tried to avoid redundancies among staff and cutbacks in student numbers have increasingly turned to the MSC for funds and have therefore adopted MSC syllabusses. This change of control and emphasis in education is crucial as it reverses the advances fought for by staff and students in the 1960s and 1970s to increase the educational content of syllabuses. Teachers now find themselves teaching 'life skills' and work experience while students have opportunities for general education cut away. But they may, if they are lucky, get on to a course about microelectronics.

## A top priority area

Several official and quasi-official state agencies are involved in sponsoring courses on microelectronics. The Training Services division of the MSC is the most important through its involvement with colleges of further education and the Industrial Training Boards. In fact, training in microelectronics has been allocated top priority. The target of financing courses to train 1,500 programmers and systems analysts in 1978-9 has been expanded to 3,500 in 1980-81. The MSC aims to supplement the supply of electronics workers and technicians being trained with industry. Courses at the Skillcentres are being redesigned to include microelectronics. MSC-supported courses in colleges of further education are also being revamped in co-operation with the Technical Education Council

(TEC) which has responsibility for science and technical qualifications below university degree standard. There are at present four TEC ordinary certificates that are equivalent to the old Ordinary National Certificate and Diploma. Fourteen TEC higher certificates equivalent to the old Higher National Certificate and Diploma are running or being developed in microelectronics. All these courses are on top of the independent initiatives taken by each College. And the number of students is expected to rise from 164 in 1979-80 to 453 in 1981-8.

## National Computing Centre

The National Computing Centre (NCC), based in Manchester, provides two types of training in microelectronics. It was appointed by the Department of Industry to administer the Microprocessor Applications Project that is aimed at making engineers already in industry aware of the potential of microelectronics. Established training bodies were invited to submit proposals for new courses. Hatfield Polytechnic, for instance, has signed a two-year contract with the NCC to provide equipment and staff for 25 ten-day courses taking 750 students. The NCC provides 50% of the £160,000 needed for the courses through the MAP money.

In all the NCC allocated £3.2 million up to the end of February 1980 in 133 grants mainly for short courses.

*Table 14.2* Grants under the MAP scheme provided through the NCC

| Institutions | Grants |
|---|---|
| Universities | 27 |
| Polytechnics | 25 |
| Local Education Authority Colleges | 45 |
| Private Sector Training | 22 |
| Others | 14 |
| Total | 133 |

The NCC also administers two computer programming and operating schemes. 'Initial Programmer' is for employer-sponsored students and lasts for 42 weeks split up into nine weeks in college, eight at work, another nine in college followed by a 16-week project in industry. The entry requirement is for four O Levels and when completed students get a Technical Education Council certificate in computer studies.

'Initial Programmer' is funded by the Manpower Services Commission through the Industrial Training Boards. The 'Threshold' scheme, the NCC's second course, is funded directly through the MSC. It is aimed at unqualified, unemployed school leavers and young people in dead-end jobs. The scheme was started in 1977 and the numbers have grown rapidly from about 180 programmers and operators in the first year to 1,200 in 1979-80.

Once students have been through these schemes they have no guarantee of employment and they are attracting a luke-warm reception from employers who either do not want to release young workers for training or prefer to recruit already trained workers.

The industrial training Boards have also had their role to play in turning education into training. As well as being a pipeline for the 'Initial Programmer' scheme funds, the Boards have reviewed their own activities to get them into line with the rest of training and its emphasis on microelectronics.

The biggest, the Engineering Training Board, published its review of microelectronic training requirements and urged management to understand the impact microelectronics will have on industrial processes and design. Skill shortages identified by the Board following the development of microelectronics include technicians, professional engineers and computer staff. Part of the Board's programme of action is to help in setting up local workshops where managers from engineering companies 'will be able to come together and consider the manpower and training implications of the application of microelectronics'.

The Board is also providing funds, to the tune of £70 a week, for each professional engineer or technologist released for post-graduate studies. Machine tool technology at Birmingham University and digital computer techniques at Strathclyde are just two examples of the courses taken. Companies can also claim £70 a week for sending what the Board calls 'mature employees' on systems analyst and programming courses that last for ten weeks at Further Education Colleges and Polytechnics.

# 15
# Alternative Design

Traditionally shopfloor trade union opposition to new technologies has usually taken the form of a blanket refusal to operate the new machinery, or a demand for more money for doing so, and an attempt to minimise job loss.

While the Luddite approach – the refusal to work new machines – has been dramatically successful in the short-term, in the long-term it has had to be modified, with some compromise involving job loss and changed job organisation being accepted. On the whole, workers in Britain have been relatively successful in resisting the harmful effects of new technologies: job loss, the loss of traditional skills, the speed-up of work with increased physical and mental stress, the loss of immediate job control. Perhaps this is because the British working class had a much stronger dose of technological change very early on, during the industrial revolution.

One of the results of this success has been the refusal by companies to invest in British industries and the export of investment capital overseas. As the very existence of a class of capitalists depends on the productivity of labour, capital will be exported to or invested wherever that productivity is greatest. The investment strike in Britain by multinational companies is the clearest statement of the organisational strength of the working class.

But what does this mean in the age of microelectronics? We are told constantly on the TV and in the papers that other countries are racing ahead of Britain in the application of microelectronic technology, that Britain is falling behind and that this will lead to economic ruin – 'Britain won't be able to compete in world markets'. Does this mean, if it is true, that we should drop all resistance to new technologies, forget the two centuries of workers' experience of technical change since the start of the industrial revolution, and quietly agree to all microelectronic-controlled technology?

## What demands?

Clearly our answer is no. This we are already acting on; but what demands should be pressed in this increasingly technological age? Most agree on the demand for more money to operate new equipment and for no loss of jobs; but even here there are problems. New machines, particularly computer-controlled ones, so dramatically increase the productivity of labour that even a £10 a week pay increase is small compared with the increase in productivity. On job loss, many employers may agree to a no-redundancy agreement, but natural wastage will be the most common method used by employers to shed labour as it has in the past. Although we should also be aware that management in some industries — steel, textiles — is using the excuse of the world recession and falling demand to cut jobs that have already, or are about to be replaced by new machinery, often computer-controlled.

It is clear that natural wastage has serious implications for youth employment. The fact is, if jobs disappear altogether with few new jobs being created, then only those few young people who are highly trained with relevant skills will find it easy to get a job after school. Women workers are seriously affected by natural wastage in ways that are different from men. When job loss is effected by natural wastage, women who leave waged employment to have children will most likely find their jobs have disappeared. In some of the industries, for example, food, beverages, light assembly, that are most likely to be affected by microelectronics, women work part-time — what does the demand for a shorter working week, based as it is on forty hours plus overtime, mean for part-timers?

By demanding higher wages and refusing job loss, workers safeguard living standards and in some way force the question of new technology out into the open; but are these enough? Many trade unions, trade union education departments in colleges and the TUC have responded by organising courses for workers, discussing the possibilities of New Technology Agreements, technology stewards and looking at the implications for bargaining, union organisation at plant and national level.

## Control of design

There is something else that critically affects the outcome of struggle with employers over the use of new technologies: the design process. Multinational companies, including the huge electronics firms like IBM, control the systems design of all computerised systems they sell or operate. The implications of this for workers can be seen in the application of any computer system in *any* workplace.

In the Coal Industry, deskilling—the down-grading and reduction of skill levels—has been deliberately designed into the whole Minos system (Chapter 10). Top management, the top systems designers and electronic and engineering firms acting as outside contractors have all had a part to play in this. The National Coal Board's aim—a massive increase in productivity—means they must tackle the problem of the human labourer, either his very existence, or his immediate control over the work process.

Frederick Lamond, a data processing (dp) specialist, writing a report on the French Government's series of public teach-ins on 'Computers and Society', makes some interesting comments about systems design (*Computing*, February 21, 1980). After noting examples of 'oppressive' systems design given by conference participants, he adds: 'One system that was not described at the French Teach-in . . . was the company word processing system designed by a US dp analyst, which proposed depriving all executives of their personal secretaries and replacing these by dictating machines, while the secretaries were put in a "word processing pool", to process the dictating machine cassettes and thus "optimise the use of word processing equipment". . .Now who is responsible for such alienating and enslaving computer system design?' Lamond then reports a comment by a revolutionary socialist, who says: 'Computers are morally neutral tools, which can be used for good or ill. But in the hands of an oppressive social system they cannot be used but for oppressive purposes'.

Lamond replies in his article: 'The truth is altogether less comfortable than that . . . alienating and oppressive computer systems have been designed first and foremost by computer professionals'. He then goes on to blame himself and other computer professionals for doing this all by themselves, largely in an effort to prove just what clever systems they can design.

Two questions emerge: Is technology neutral; if it is not, who controls it, who designs in the bias?

The type of training and education that engineers and designers get includes a very large part of management science, and many of the other disciplines that they learn are also directed by managerial philosophies. Designers learn to incorporate certain design approaches and values during their training. But if the designers are biased does this necessarily mean that the technology is also not neutral?

While chips and other parts that make up computer hardware may be neutral, just as an electric motor driving an assembly line is neutral, the functioning system, whether it is a computer system or an assembly line, is not neutral and has deliberately been designed in oppressive ways. Managerial authority and control is placed inside technical systems, which may, in fact be quite small – the tachograph in a lorry cab – or quite large – a car assembly line. Either way the technology controls and paces the workers involved.

## Worker designers and alternative systems design

The Health and Safety at Work Act (HSWA), 1974, gave trade union safety stewards certain legal rights. Many stewards in well-organised workplaces already had most of these rights – like the right to make regular inspections, the right to information – but the huge majority of stewards did not. This legislation, however limited in scope it may be, was only won with a hard struggle, which took many years of effort. With good shopfloor organisation, these legal rights can be extended and used in far-reaching ways: the space has been created in which a movement is growing. Rank and file health and safety groups have grown up in most major cities, as have hazards groups of technical workers, within the British Society for Social Responsibility in Science.

Can this Act, however, be used to extend the rights of the shopfloor representatives to include the right of direct, local negotiation over the design of plant and equipment? The HSWA says employers must provide safe systems of work as well as safe equipment and processes. This system of work clearly would include new computerised systems – an NCB Coal Preparation Plant, or an industrial robot in a foundry or a word processing system in an office. We can look very closely at the particular safety problems involved in any of these and especially at the problem of *stress*, a hazard much neglected by health and safety workers until recently.

However, this still does not get at the heart of the problem – the design of the overall work process, or important parts of it; nor does it address the problem of management control of this design process. The HSWA also requires employers to take due regard of the welfare of employees as well as their health and safety, but does this mean the provision of interesting, skilled work rather than boring, monotonous, unskilled drudgery? Clearly, with most employers, especially under a Conservative government, arguments over welfare will not have much effect.

The TUC is considering the idea of New Technology Agreements, backed up by New Technology Stewards. This idea is borrowed from Norway, where this kind of organisation has already been adopted by the trades unions. However, there are some serious pitfalls in this approach. Some of the pitfalls are similar to those that appeared with the HSWA and the appointment of Safety Representatives. Many unions have decided that, instead of setting up a new and separate lay position, existing stewards will also be safety representatives and will receive the training that the unions have been offered. Again, while in the early days some unions negotiated Safety Agreements with employers, this has often been dropped as, in many cases cases, workers ended up with fewer rights than they actually had in law.

Technological issues, as with safety issues, must be negotiable, and the negotiations, from the union side, must include as many shopfloor representatives as is necessary. There are clear dangers, and these have occurred in Norway, with the appointment of New Technology Stewards (NTS) and the signing of New Technology Agreements. The stewards can become isolated and drift away from the hard issues of shopfloor organisation. Agreements, on the other hand, also tend to isolate away from the central bargaining process, issues that are intimately related to many constant shopfloor problems, worker/machine levels, training and pace of work.

What is really needed on the shop- and office-floor is a movement of worker-designers, similar to that of safety representatives. Design is a highly technical process, so how can shop- or office-floor workers make any effective input into the design process—let alone argue with management specialists like computer systems designers and electronic and production engineers?

What we must remember before getting into a discussion of this kind, is that systems design is first and foremost a political or organisational activity rather than a merely technical one. Very many engineers, especially junior engineers, have as little understanding of the aims of chief systems designers as have shopfloor union representatives who are not even involved in the design team. This is because the key decisions over levels of skills, numbers of workers, total computer control or an aid to workers are taken by top managers alone. Shopfloor representatives in many instances understand the politics of the workplace far better than any top manager because they work inside the process day in and day out.

For these reasons, the fact that shopfloor representatives have no input, control or negotiating rights at the level of design is of central importance. Lack of technical knowledge is not of secondary importance. If it is true that we are moving towards a society where workers will be trained and retrained several times in their lives because of technical change, and towards a society with fewer jobs, then the first type of training that we can demand, along with paid time off, is training in technology.

## The Swedish Work Environment Act

In the late 1970s, a number of Scandinavian countries greatly extended the statutory rights of safety representatives. The Work Environment Act 1978 in Sweden gave safety representatives the legal right to be involved in the design and planning process from the first stages. Employers cannot get building permits for new factories or offices unless the Factory Inspectorate has seen signed statements from union representatives declaring that they have been involved in the design of the new premises. Swedish safety representatives are taught on new courses how to demand particular workplace design information, just as a number of years ago, health and safety courses taught safety representatives how to approach the highly technical problems of hazards at work like chemical hazards. Not only can Swedish safety representatives check new technologies for basic safety problems (like eyestrain while using visual display units), but they can also insist, prior to installation and during design and development, that jobs whose skill levels are to be changed are *re*skilled rather than *de*skilled. They can demand that monotony is reduced and that no worker is socially isolated by a work process. They therefore have a fundamental right to argue over the quality of their working environment, something that is intimately related to the question of basic job organisation.

While the main struggle at the workplace is necessarily over wages and jobs, shopfloor representatives who have a statutory right to be involved in health, safety and design questions will be able to place themselves in a much more powerful position to fight for wages and jobs. They will also be able to prevent the decimation of union organisation that is quite often part and parcel of technical change. In addition, the central political question of the times—productivity —can be dealt with far more effectively. No longer will it simply be a question of accepting or rejecting productivity bargaining, for example. They would have a great deal more room to manoeuvre in, and in fact the argument could be re-established on a different terrain.

However, like any other right, a statutory right to be able to argue and negotiate over design and planning is only meaningful if the strength is there on the shopfloor to use it, to insist that it is expanded, and to prevent it from being taken away. With this kind of right, and backed by the strong union organisation they *do* have,

South Kirkby miners and the NUM as a whole could demand that the closed loop system not be used in Minos. They could demand some type of open loop system, where workers maintain their job control.

While Britain is neither Sweden nor Norway, and while British employers are not as liberal as Scandinavian management, if the design issue is not raised then only two choices are left: adamant refusal to operate new machinery, or near enough complete acquiescence to it, with all that that entails. To protect jobs, skills, job organisation and maintain and increase standards of living then the argument and negotiation over design, development, installation and the operation of new technology must begin.

## Robots or Telechirics?

The Lucas Aerospace Shop Stewards Combine has shown how arguments over design can be effective when applied to products. The Combine has researched and designed socially useful products like heat pumps and telechiric machines. It has demanded that Lucas start manufacturing these to save jobs, and also in place of military hardware. In pressing for the development of telechiric machinery the Combine is intervening in the systems design process as it affects other workers who will use these machines. Telechiric machines used in a work process are high technology systems using microelectronics, but completely controlled by the workers who operate them. They are already being used in very dangerous jobs and they could also be used in other work processes.

It is likely, however, that more and more industrial workers are going to be faced with the prospect of robots, not telechirics, in the short term. What is the effective response to an announcement that robots will be installed on such and such a job in so many months?

At BL, Longbridge, there is already a struggle over who is going to program, and thus control, the robots that BL wants to install. At Datsun, in Japan, in a completely different industrial relations climate, workers have been taught how to program the robots in the welding shop. So what are the possibilities?

Robots are good at selecting parts from pre-position parts feeders and moving them to assembly areas as well as carrying out welding and paint spraying jobs. Actual assembly by robots is coming; what is quite crucial is that, where robots and workers work on jobs in common, workers can control the pace at which the robots work, rather than vice versa. There is no reason why workers should not become programmer-teachers of robot systems; this would keep immediate job control on the shopfloor. One possibility is a master-slave control, similar to that used in telechiric systems, with the worker using it every time a new job is to be set up. In a co-operative worker-robot system, the worker could define what s/he wants the robot to do by using the master-slave control, and what s/he wants to do her/himself.

While many union organisations at the local and shop steward level do not share the advantages of the Lucas Combine which includes engineers and designers as well as other workers, there are an increasing number of socialist technologists who could help shopfloor unions develop counter-proposals in design. Unions should also employ or use these specialised workers, rather than depending on 'independent' consultancy companies, whose personnel have almost always had a firm managerial training. Special courses, not just of the two- or five-day release type, must also be organised for shopfloor representatives, and should be set up in good trade union studies departments, or organised from union schools directly. In this way shopfloor representatives will be able to apply their daily experience of technologies to a more technical level of information. If shopfloor representatives have the base of a strong plant-union organisation, they can rely primarily on their own rich experience, supplemented by technical knowledge. The first problem is always organisation, the second, knowledge, but really the two are inseparable in everyday life at work.

### The tachograph – battle over technical surveillance at work

The tachograph was originally designed by Herbert Kienzle, a German instrument maker, and used in the 1920s to record the productivity of workers not only in lorries, but also those working at certain machines in factories. The first models may seem crude by today's standards, but the modern tachograph, in spite of what European Economic Commissioners might say about it, remains an instrument of management control, and is sold as such by manufacturers. Kienzle and some Japanese companies have developed a micro-electronic controlled tachograph, but as the EEC legislation is built around the circular chart for recording information, rather than electronic memory, this device is still some way off in Europe.

Drivers in Britain have long resisted this productivity device, dubbing it 'the spy-in-the-cab', and from earlier experiences with the Service Recorder of the 1920s, they have remained convinced that the real purpose of tachographs has always been as a productivity device, rather than as an instrument for road safety. From the first strike action taken against the introduction of tachographs in 1969 they were banned by workers. Although a ballot of drivers in 1979 was lost, the huge majority of drivers still do not want the tachograph. The 1979 ballot was lost for a number of reasons. The main one was the fact that many drivers had only recently taken part in the national lorry strike the previous winter. The winter strike, the first ever national lorry strike, was made official after the rank and file had made it a national fact. The Transport and General Workers Union leadership dreaded an even more serious affair over the tachograph. From a tactical point of view it wasn't the time to face the newly elected Tory government. But then again, the working class cannot always choose the time.

The modern tachograph is the culmination of a whole series of design choices, stretching over a sixty year period, during which the people whom it most directly affects were never involved. This lack of involvement is not surprising for two reasons: first, there is the traditional exclusion of workers from design; but second, there is the understanding on the part of many workers involved that the tachograph is essentially a repressive piece of technology, of only negative value for workers.

However, the ballot on industrial action against the 1979 government legislation has been lost and the tachograph will now be installed in 600,000 vehicles in the United Kingdom. The period of unqualified rejection has come to an end; the question must be handled in a different way. As a result, the National Committee of the Road Haulage group within the TGWU has decided that, if the tachograph is going to be accepted, then the letter of the law will be followed. When the date arrives for the national changeover from drivers' log books to the use of tachograph charts, on completion of their charts, drivers will hand over the charts into the safe-keeping of the senior steward at the depot, rather than the transport manager. Management will not have access to the tremendous amount of managerial information on each chart. Although this is a second-best solution to the tachograph problem, from the drivers' viewpoint it will safeguard them from the greatly increased exploitation the tachograph was originally designed for.

A lot of computer applications, especially now that cheap and adaptable microelectronics abound, have built into them a subsystem for worker monitoring and pacing. These are universally applied, in offices, mines, factories, chemical plants. Microelectronics provides the basis for excellent monitoring devices and can be set to monitor workers' productivity — work rates, stoppages, rest breaks—as easily as temperature, liquid flow rate, mechanical movements or other technical factors. Wherever the worker-monitoring systems are incorporated, whether it is in a Ford factory with VDUs at every foreman's desk, or a supermarket check-out machine with built-in productivity monitor of the check-out operator, these functions can be *designed out* and should be.

The more these workplace surveillance systems are used, then the more like robots workers will become and the more like workers robots will become—a unity of people and machine in robotisation. The reality is that managers constantly seek to measure people, materials and machines in the same terms, through the use of modern, synthetic time and motion study systems like Methods Time Measurement. This and other time study methods are programmed into on-line worker-monitoring systems. Quite a number of workers do not realise that this is what is happening until it is far too late to act.

Engineers and designers like to pretend that they make design choices solely on technical grounds. Experience and training teach us that this is not true. The typical hierarchy of control set up in modern applications of computer systems is not technically necessary. As in the NCB Minos system and many similar systems in other workplaces, the new electronic hardware and software is organised to mimic and even intensify traditional top-down management. It is neither technically necessary nor is it technically inevitable to have such hierarchies of power in the workplace. In fact as microelectronics can control a piece of equipment independently of other machines, the technical structure of work could be made much more democratic, less centralised and less hierarchical. Workers can demand that the systems designers specify their objectives in *advance* for each of the worker-machine systems. It is possible to *negotiate* over the type of skills and job control at each of these levels in the hierarchy, so as to remove most of the hierarchy itself.

# Further Reading

### Capitalism & Technology

This chapter draws extensively on Marx's *Capital*, which is best studied in a reading group. For an introduction see:

Karl Marx, *Wages, Prices and Profit*, or

Geoff Kay, *The Economic Theory of the Working Class*, (Macmillan, 1979.

The Capitalist organisation of the labour process is discussed in Harry Braverman, *Labour and Monopoly Capital* (Monthly Review Press, 1974).

### Chapter 5 Office

Jane Barker and Hazel Downing, 'Word Processing and the Transformation of the Patriarchal Relations of Control in the Office', in *Capital and Class*, Number 10 (CSE, 1980). This includes an extensive bibliography.

Mary Kathleen Benet, *Secretary: An Enquiry into the Female Ghetto* (Sidgwick and Jackson, 1972).

### Chapter 6 Small Batch Production

Coventry Workshop, *Crisis in Engineering: Machine Tools' Workers Fight for Jobs* (Institute for Workers' Control, Nottingham, 1979).

D. Noble, 'Social Choice in Machine Design: The Case of Automatically Controlled Machine Tools', in A. Zimbalist (ed.), *Case Studies in the Labour Process* (Monthly Review Press, 1979).

### Chapter 13 Education

N. J. Rushby, *An Introduction to Educational Computing*, (Croom Helm, 1979). A full, thoughtful description of the current state-of-the-art.

### Chapter 14 Training

Dan Finn, 'The Rise of Manpower Servicedom', in Centre for Contemporary Cultural Studies, *Unpopular Education: Schooling and Social Democracy* (Hutchinson, 1980, forthcoming).

Simon Frith, 'Education, Training and the Labour Process' (CSE Education Group, 1978).

## CSE Books

CSE Books was founded by members of the Conference of Socialist Economists to promote the practical criticism of capitalism which the CSE as a whole is committed to and to facilitate wider participation in the debate and analysis going on in the CSE. Rather than forming ourselves into an academic editorial committee which sits in judgement of authors and in ignorance of readers, we want to engage politically in current debates and struggles. By coordinating with CSE activities in general, by publishing *Head & Hand: A Socialist Review of Books*, and by organising dayschools on issues thrown up by our own publications, we hope to narrow the gap which exists in bourgeois society between the producers and consumers of books.

For further information on CSE Books titles and the CSE Book club, write to 55 Mount Pleasant, London WC1X 0AE.

## New Titles

*Living Thinkwork: Where Do Labour Processes Come From?* Mike Hales.
Mike Hales describes his experience doing operations research at ICI where even mental workers learn that ultimately 'You're not paid to think'. Through an account of 'scientific' work in a capitalist firm his book shows the place of knowledge-production in the politics of management. A concrete intervention in Marxist theory of the labour process, this book is also a document in the history of the 'class of '68', exploring the contradictory social relations between theory and personal experience, theory and practice, and academic and industrial work. 192 pages illust.
Hb 0 906336 14 7 £10/Pb 0 906336 15 5 £3.50.

*Northern Ireland: Between Civil Rights and Civil War*, Liam O'Dowd, Bill Rolston & Mike Tomlinson.
This book is the first major study to document the origins and nature of Direct Rule in Northern Ireland, particularly the social democratic model which Britain has attempted to superimpose upon the Orange State. The authors argue that Direct Rule has not been overcoming the notorious sectarianism of Stormont but has instead reconstituted class sectarian relations more subtly within the new state institutions. Their argument is illustrated through detailed studies of the economy, trade unions, local government, housing community politics and repression.
Hb 0 906336 18 X £12/Pb 0 906336 19 8 £3.95.

*Science, Technology and the Labour Process: Marxist Studies*, volume I. Ed. Les Levidow & Bob Young. (Autumn 1980). This series of collections will analyse scientific and technological practices in terms of the capitalist labour process, especially the current restructuring of capital. The articles in the first volume take up the following areas: mental labour, microelectronics, Marx on technology, genetic engineering, Grunwick's fixed capital and scientific conceptualisation.
Hb 0 906336 20 1/Pb 0 906336 21 X.

*Value: The Representation of Labour in Capitalism*, ed. Diane Elson. Marx's theory of value has been a controversial and constant matter of debate since the time it was first published. This collection of essays focuses on some of the more difficult and neglected concepts at the very beginning of *Capital*: abstract labour as the substance of value; the relative and equivalent forms of value; exchange value as a necessary mode of expression of value; the commodity as a symbol. The book also contains a useful annotated bibliography of all Marx's references to value. 192 pages.
Hb 0 906336 07 4 £12.00 / Pb 0 906336 08 2 £4.95

## The Conference of Socialist Economists

The Conference of Socialist Economists was formed in 1970. Since that time there have been many changes. CSE is committed to the development of a materialist critique of capitalism in the Marxist tradition. The membership of CSE now covers a broad spectrum of political and research activities which generates a wide-ranging debate, for CSE is as far as possible, unconstrained by the traditional academic divisions of intellectual labour into, say, 'economics', 'politics', 'sociology', or 'history'.

Instead the groupings are around the CSE working groups. Currently, groups actively working on material are the Ideology Group, Housing, Capital and the State, State Economic Policy, Capitalist Labour Process, Political Economy of Women, European Integration, Health and Social Policy. There is a Labour Process Historians' Group and there may at different times be other groups in operation. Groups are in various parts of the country.

For further information on membership, write to CSE, 55 Mount Pleasant, London WC1X 0AE.

Also available from CSE Books

*Technology and Toil in Nineteenth Century Britain*, ed. Maxine Be
A collection of documents designed to illustrate the neglected ea
history of deskilling, technological unemployment and assembly li
alienation. The fifty-one selections reveal differing practices in a wi
range of industries and provide a context in which the better kno
analyses of work and technology left by Babbage, Ure, Owen and Ma
may be analysed. 250 pages illust.
Hb 0 906336 02 3 £10.00 / Pb 0 906336 03 1 £3.50.

*Economy and Class Structure of German Fascism*, Alfred Sohn-Reth
A classic Marxist study of the founding of the Nazi state in the ea
1930s. Sohn-Rethel managed to infiltrate the office of the Mitt
europaeischer Wirtschaftstag, a business institute whose members
cluded representatives of every significant section of German fina
capital, and the book is based on his experiences as an editorial assist
on the MWT's newsletter. 160 pages.
Hb 0 906336 00 7 £5.95 / Pb 0 906336 01 5 £2.50.

*Struggle Over the State*, CSE State Group
Building on the current upsurge of Marxist interest in the state, t
collectively produced work combines recent theoretical progress w
informed and up-to-date description of the restructuring of the
state in the crisis of the 1970s. 144 pages illust.
Hb 0 906336 13 9 £5.95 / Pb 0 906336 12 0 £2.50.

*Working Class Autonomy and the Crisis: Italian Marxist Texts of
Theory and Practice of a Class Movement 1964-79*. (Joint publicat
with Red Notes).
The core of this book is a new Marxist politics, a new conception
revolutionary working class organisation—both integrated with
changing composition of the working class from 1962 to the pres
day. Contains first-time translations of articles by Mario Tronti, Se
Bologna and Toni Negri (including the work which immedia
preceded his arrest, 'Capitalist Domination and Working C
Sabotage'). A4 size, 206 pages illust.
0 906305 05 5 £3.95.

*A Workers' Enquiry into the Motor Industry*, IWC Motors Group.
Examines redundancies, speed-ups, payments systems, automat
health and safety, and the international reorganisation of capital inv
ment—all from the point of view of labour. A4 size, 102 pages illust
0 906336 05 8 £2.25.